REMINISCENCES

BY

J. SCOTT LIDGETT, M.A., D.D.

Author of *Sonship and Salvation, The Christian Religion: Its Meaning and Proof, The Fatherhood of God,* &c.

WIPF & STOCK · Eugene, Oregon

Wipf and Stock Publishers
199 W 8th Ave, Suite 3
Eugene, OR 97401

Reminiscences
By Lidgett, J. Scott
Copyright©1928 Methodist Publishing - Epworth Press
ISBN 13: 978-1-5326-3838-1
Publication date 7/27/2017
Previously published by Epworth Press, 1928

PREFACE

THE following pages have already appeared in a series of articles contributed to *The Methodist Magazine*. When the Editor very kindly invited me to write them, on the completion of fifty years of ministry in the Wesleyan Methodist Church, I was, at first, taken completely aback. I had had no thought of leaving any record behind, though I had prepared a careful memorandum on the origin and history of the Bermondsey Settlement for the use of my successor. Yet, after reflection, I felt that some of my memories of men and movements might be worthy of a permanent record and might be of service to those who come after. In particular, I hoped that my account of the Bermondsey Settlement might lead to fuller and wider knowledge of the importance of its work, and so to its preservation in time to come as, under present conditions, an indispensable instrument of social well-being in one of the poorest districts of London. So I consented to write, and these Reminiscences are the result.

The narrative might easily have been expanded and amplified, but I decided that it should be just a brief and simple tale of the outstanding facts and experiences of my life and work. As such I am content to leave it in the hope that it may be of interest and service, especially to the younger ministers of the Church.

J. SCOTT LIDGETT.

Easter, 1928.

CONTENTS

REMINISCENCES

I.

ANCESTRY AND EARLY INFLUENCES

Paternal Grandparents.

IT is necessary for me to begin by saying something of my ancestry. Both my paternal grandparents were brought up in the Established Church; but both came under strong religious influences in early life, and were led to find in Methodism the spiritual fellowship in which their Christian life could best be strengthened and developed. My grandfather, John Lidgett, born in Hull in the year 1800, was of mixed aristocratic and commercial, of partly English and partly Scottish, descent, his grandmother being a Pierrepont and related to the then Duke of Kingston; another ancestor being a MacIntosh, who was slain fighting for Prince Charlie in 1745.

Left fatherless in his early boyhood, John Lidgett felt the lure of the sea, and became a sailor, rising to the command of a vessel in his early twenties, and becoming subsequently a successful shipowner in the City of London. While preparing to go to sea, the boy had been laid hold of by ' Daddy ' Post, an old Methodist gate-keeper at the Hull Docks, who lay in wait for the boys who frequented the Docks, in order to bring them to religious decision. This encounter (for so at first it was) became the turning-point of his history; for my grandfather, while characterized throughout his life by great courage, enterprise, and business capacity, became, above all, a saint. To say this is not to be guilty of exaggeration. I well remember his transfigured countenance when I was taken to his deathbed in 1861, and he bade me ' meet him in heaven.'

On reaching the Port of London, after one of his early voyages, my grandfather met with his future wife, Anne Hyett, of Gloucester, who had come to London to fare for herself in consequence of family opposition on her having ' turned Methodist.' She was of Huguenot descent. An ancestor, Augustin Courtauld, came to England at the Revocation of the Edict of Nantes. His grand-daughter married into the family of Jacob, who came over from Metz later on. Eventually their grand-daughter married into the family of Hyett, a member of which was Constable of Gloucester and represented the County in Parliament from 1722 to 1727. The family was also related to John Moore, who was Archbishop of Canterbury from 1783 to 1805.

Owing to causes that I need not narrate, my grandmother's parents were in reduced circumstances, and my grandmother endured some hardness in her youth. She was a remarkable woman, adding to her deep religious convictions great vivacity, keen and wide intellectual interests, and, not least of all, intense ambition, not so much for the material prosperity as for the education and intellectual development, first of her children, and afterwards of her grandchildren. In this last respect, the high and exacting standards she set before me, as well as the stimulating effect of her conversation, have exerted a lifelong influence upon me.

Maternal Grandparents.

My maternal grandfather, John Scott, was the son of a farmer at Copmanthorpe, near York. His mother, who had heard John Wesley, had become an earnest Methodist, and at an early age he entered the Wesleyan Methodist ministry in 1811. Endowed with deep devotion, great dignity of character, and remarkable sagacity, he early became a trusted lieutenant of Dr. Bunting, exercised a moderating influence in the painful controversies of 1849, and was twice President of the Conference—in 1843 and in 1852. A constructive ecclesiastical statesman in the best sense, he was concerned in every department of Methodism and in every policy of Connexional advance. His most eminent services, however, were in the sphere of Education. Those were the days when the need of popular education was convincing the mind and stirring the conscience of Christian people in all denominations. Following upon the establishment of ' National ' and ' British ' Schools, the Wesleyan Conference set out to found a system of its own. A Connexional Education Committee was appointed, and John Scott was its Chairman from 1843 to the time of his death at the beginning of 1868. By his efforts Westminster College was built, and he became its Principal throughout the eventful years when Wesleyan Day Schools were being founded in all parts of the country.

At Westminster John Scott became the head of a remarkable band of colleagues, whose devotion to the cause of Education was so vital a part of their Christian consecration that they regarded their work as a sacred calling in the strictest sense. Among these, perhaps William Sugden, James Bailey, and Charles Mansford are the best remembered. Drawing was taught by James Smetham the artist, whose published letters are likely to become a literary classic and whose deep spirituality coloured all his art. The health of the College was committed to the care of William Kitchin Parker, subsequently F.R.S. and Hunterian Professor of Anatomy, the friend and fellow-worker of Huxley, who combined, in his eager spirit and restless mind, an early acceptance of Darwinism, concentrated and highly skilful efforts to work the doctrine out and verify it in embryology, with the deep and satisfying enjoyment of the Wesleyan Hymn-Book and the Class-Meeting, in which he took refuge from the intellectual difficulties of scientific speculation.

Matthew Arnold was the Government Inspector of the College, and was in close contact with my grandfather. Only a few years ago an educationist who was engaged in searching out the history of Elementary Education in the Early Victorian period, inquired of me whether I was related to John Scott; and when I told him that I was his grandson, he informed me that, in searching the records at the Board of Education, he found what a great part John Scott had played, and that, whenever a suggestion was made either by or to Matthew Arnold, he had been accustomed to remark, ' I must consult Scott about it.' The deep impression made by him in educational affairs was described by the late Lord Thring in a letter to Dr. Rigg, which is published in the Life of the Latter (p. 167.)

Only recently I had fresh evidence of the outstanding qualities of this work. The Secretary of the Consultative Committee of the Board of Education applied to me for information as to the time-tables in Wesleyan Schools during the fifties and early sixties of last century, which he had been told by Sir Michael Sadler were of special importance. I had the pleasure of calling attention to John Scott's Inaugural Address, delivered to the Westminster students in 1862, when the Right Hon. Robert Lowe, in the interests of so-called economy, was seeking to restrict the development of Elementary Education, and, for that purpose, to establish the baneful system of payment by results.

This address, which was formally adopted and published by the Wesleyan Education Committee, has the heading, ' The Working Classes Entitled to a Good Education.' In the course of it my grandfather declared ' that the education provided in Wesleyan Schools *must be good,* and that it cannot be *too good* for those who are to receive it.' He asked with indignation, ' Must that largest class of children, to whom '' the Lord, the Maker of them all '' has given capabilities equal in every respect to the children of the classes above them, be restricted to something much humbler than this generous ideal of education? ' He claimed that in this matter Wesleyans would ' prove themselves to be, as they have ever been, the true friends of the people.' ' If,' he added, ' the improvement in the humbler classes obliges the middle and even the higher classes to do something further for their own elevation in the social scale, the Wesleyans will the more rejoice.' So he reached his italicized conclusion,—' That as good an education should be given to the poor as their children can receive.' The whole address is so modern and progressive in its outlook that I have more than once made extensive quotations from it in School Board and subsequent educational contests. From time to time, throughout all the years of my ministry, it has been my joy to meet with men and women who have told me how much they owed to his personal guidance and wise counsels.

My maternal grandmother, Maria Scott, was the daughter of a Sheffield manufacturer. In her early life she had been a favourite of Dr. Adam Clarke. Owing to this and to her later associations, she was a storehouse of information as to the leading personalities of Methodism from the closing years of Wesley onwards. Her striking beauty had been marred by years of intense suffering, due largely to the climate of Westminster, and borne with marvellous fortitude and patience. On removal to our home at Blackheath after her husband's death, she quickly recovered, and in tranquillity was wont to pour out these personal memories for the benefit of her grandchildren. The great names of Adam Clarke, Richard Watson, James Dixon, Robert Newton, and a host more were household words.

Influences that Shaped my Early Life.

It was under the influences I have described that my early life was shaped and my outlook determined. My father, John Jacob Lidgett, inherited to the full all the high qualities of his parents. A successful man of business, he divided his leisure between pursuits of mental culture and works of church service and Christian philanthropy. Broad in outlook and unspeakably tender, he was buoyant in spirit, full of wit and humour, eloquent in speech, and wonderfully tactful, though firm, in his handling of men and affairs. He had made his mark as a coming man in the counsels of Methodism, and was expected to play a distinguished part in public affairs, when premature death came to him in 1869, before I was fifteen years of age. At his passing, men who had known him in the City remarked, ' If ever there were a Christian in business, he was one.' On the eve of my entering the ministry my mother informed me that it had been my father's constant prayer that God would call me to this work.

My mother, never robust in health, though she lived to a great age, helped to found and eventually became President of what is now the Women's Department of the Missionary Society. To this she gave all the attention that could be spared from the claims of home and hospitality. Widowed at a time of considerable financial uncertainty, she made me the confidant of her anxieties, and thus I grew up, somewhat heavily weighted in my later 'teens by religious influences and domestic concerns.

The effects of these relationships upon my early life were very great. To begin with, I was brought up in the inner circle of the Wesleyan ministry. Taken as an infant to the deathbed of Dr. Bunting to receive his blessing, I was brought into frequent contact with the outstanding ministers of the Connexion. When I became President of the Conference in 1908, I studied the list of my predecessors, and discovered that I had been personally acquainted with fifty of the ninety-one individual Presidents who had held office since the death of Wesley. After I had resolved to offer myself as a candidate for the ministry, I received much valuable help, counsel, and instruction from the Revs. Dr. George Bowden, George W. Olver, and Samuel Coley. Of even greater importance was the advice given to me by Dr. W. F. Moulton and Dr. W. B. Pope in the later stages of my preparation.

In the next place, my sense of calling and my associations resulted in a certain precocity in regard to Christian work. I became a Sunday-school teacher in East Greenwich soon after I was fifteen, raised funds in the same year, chiefly from the friends of my late father, to equip the schoolroom in East Greenwich as a Wesleyan Day School, and preached my first sermon in the same building when I was sixteen and a half. At the same time I became a district visitor in one of the poorest river-side slums of East Greenwich, was made a class-leader at eighteen, and superintendent of the Blackheath Sunday School at twenty.

II.

LONDON UNIVERSITY AND MINISTRY

S O far as my education and early prospects were concerned, the death of my father placed me under the authoritative guidance of my uncle, George Lidgett, who, while deeply and affectionately concerned for my welfare, was inclined to treat his own life-history as supplying the pattern of my own. I was to become a business man in his view, and therefore I must give up my work in the Classical Sixth of the Blackheath Proprietary School at sixteen and a half. When I made known to him my sense of calling to the ministry, his decision was only strengthened; for city life would test this perhaps premature sense of vocation, and, in any case, would give me an experience of the world that would be of great advantage to a future minister. So I spent two years in a city office; and then, when my decision proved irrevocable, consent was given to my entering University College, London, where I studied for three years and a half, my uncle deciding against Oxford and Cambridge as not likely to strengthen, and perhaps likely to undermine, my Methodist convictions and sympathies.

Chief Intellectual Interest.

Having matriculated on leaving school, I went forward to my B.A. degree, and remained at the College till after I had taken the M.A. in Logic and Philosophy. I was, however, greatly hampered in the philosophical studies which became my chief intellectual interest. The Association School of the Mills and Bain was in the ascendant at the College. The very able and painstaking professor, the late G. Croom Robertson, had been appointed to the Chair in competition with Dr. Martineau, because the latter, from the very fact of his being of another philosophical School, and still more because he was the protagonist of Theism against Tyndall, Huxley, and other scientific leaders of thought, had been distasteful to the appointers. Hence I was led into an *impasse*, owing to the conflict between my religious convictions and my philosophical teachers, in which the former prevailed. Years of subsequent study and reflection were needed before I found a way of escape from this deadlock. Meanwhile the urge of practical interests was so great that I tolerated, rather than enjoyed, academic studies, being anxious to take the plunge into practical life as soon as I possibly could. It ought to be added that both the intensity of my Methodist fervour and the impact of new ideas were, to some extent, qualified by Anglican associations, while the influence of my father's sisters—very remarkable women—strengthened my natural tendency to reject the Millenarian pietism, which prevailed at Tunbridge Wells, where they lived, and to seek an interpretation of the Christian religion which gave ampler recognition to intellectual and social pursuits.

Preparation for the Ministry.

From my earliest years I had been the subject of deep religious impressions, to which a strong appeal was made by the preaching of those days, the earnestness of which was accompanied by continual insistence—disproportionate, and, as it now seems to me, somewhat unwholesome—on the Last Things. At my earnest request my grandfather gave me my first Communion at the Covenant Service of January 1868, and the next morning he was stricken by fatal illness. From that time I became a member of my uncle's Society class, and subsequently engaged in the church work to which I have referred. From the time when my call to offer for the ministry was recognized by my family, about which I will speak more fully later on, the Rev. William F. Moulton became my authoritative adviser, and his influence on my career was of continuous importance, as will be subsequently explained.

The most momentous event of my early preparation came in 1875, when I was introduced to the Rev. W. B. Pope. I had just passed the examination for the M.A. degree, and had a year of study in view before I could be accepted as a candidate by the Conference. So my uncle took me to Sheffield, where the Conference was held in 1875. There I was permitted to attend the Committees of Review, and heard the celebrated speech of Mr. Fowler (afterwards Viscount Wolverhampton) in support of Lay Representation, being able to watch the alarmed looks of the Ministerial Platform, and to hear the apprehensive comments —both public and private—of certain greatly respected Ex-Presidents. Dr. Pope received me graciously, and took me out with him for a walk in the streets of Sheffield. To my astonishment he told me that I had read sufficient doctrinal theology for the present, and counselled me to spend my strength for the coming year in studying Isaiah in Hebrew and the Epistle to the Galatians in Greek—as an introduction to the Pauline Epistles—with the best commentaries. This I did, together with the first edition of his own *Compendium of Theology,* which was published during that year.

From that time forward I enjoyed the advantage of Dr. Pope's continuous guidance and intimate conversation for the following six years. This first advice is of interest both as showing the importance assigned to Biblical Theology by the greatest of Methodist dogmatic theologians, and also as throwing light upon the workings of his own mind. In the last conversation I ever had with Dr. Pope, as we walked the streets of Southport together in 1881, he suddenly stopped and said, ' Never become a theological tutor ! If I had my time over again, I would ask to be appointed Professor of Biblical Exegesis.'

This remark was due probably in part to the natural reaction which always follows upon intense specialization, as was illustrated many years after when that prince of preachers, Dr. Maclaren of Manchester, said to me, ' If I had to begin life over again, I would take up Settlement work; it has greater practical results than preaching.' Still more, I think, it was due to the sense of the inadequacy of all human formulas to express Divine Reality, which haunted this great ' mystical dogmatist,' as Dr. J. Dury Geden once described Dr. Pope to me. This sense led him frequently to quote the saying, '*Omnia exeunt in mysterium.*' Nor was he lacking in the keen apprehension of intellectual difficulties; though, to use Newman's phrase, ' Ten thousand difficulties did not make one doubt.' I remember his inquiring of me about a lecture delivered by the Rev. F. W. Macdonald on ' The Modern Attack and Defence of the Faith ' : ' Did he show that he felt the difficulties? If not, the lecture was no good.' The impression made upon me during those years was that the leaders of Wesleyan thought were inclined to practise too much ' economy ' in the interests of safety and owing to the undue influence of a masterful personality to whom I will refer shortly.

Circuit Work and Marriage.

The Conference of 1876 accepted me as a Probationer; and as there was at that time a great demand for additional ministers I was sent at once to Tunstall, where I had a fruitful experience of a manufacturing and mining circuit. It was a shock for me, brought up in the staid atmosphere of a London suburb, to be immersed in the somewhat excitable and emotional religion that then prevailed in North Staffordshire, with its reliance upon a revivalism that was sometimes artificial and had a good many unwholesome elements. Yet I lived on terms of intimate friendship with many colliers and potters, gaining insight into their ways of thought and life, as I enjoyed their hearty hospitality. I found Wesleyan Day Schools all over the circuit, and devoted a good deal of my concern to helping the masters and mistresses, some of whom had been trained by my grandfather. I was also deeply interested in the problems of physical health, as I visited homes where hygienic conditions were sadly neglected; and this interest was stimulated by the *Life of Charles Kingsley,* which was published a few months after I arrived. But I found few to act with me in such matters, and the lack of such helpers made a deep and abiding impression upon my mind.

At the instance of Dr. W. B. Pope I was appointed to the Mornington Road Circuit, Southport, in 1878, and there I made invaluable and lasting friendships. But my heart was vexed to find so many there who had left the towns in which their wealth had been made, to enjoy an easy and somewhat aimless life at a watering-place. In the memory of Tunstall I was inclined to feel that Southport ought not to exist. The need of bringing such extremes together became a leading preoccupation of my mind. Meanwhile, though active in practical work, I was a hard student during these two appointments, always studying five and often seven hours each day.

My next appointment was at Cardiff, where the energy of a progressive and prosperous town made a great appeal to me, and where I found it much easier to enlist the services of well-to-do young people in various forms of social service. There, in addition to circuit work and building a chapel, I took a hand in many public activities, serving on the committee that established the University College, and taking a leading part in movements for combating the vice of a seaport town. Among other measures we persuaded the Town Council to embody clauses for dealing with brothels in a Municipal Bill. Difficulties having subsequently arisen, the Council decided to drop these clauses; and having with the utmost difficulty dragged a few eminent citizens with me on a deputation, I was both encouraged and amused by reading the next morning in the newspaper that ' in consequence of the strong expression of public opinion ' the Council had decided to reinstate the clauses.

In all these activities I was brought into very close relations with Dr. C. J. Vaughan, Dean of Llandaff and Master of the Temple. He threw all the weight of his great influence on the side of co-operation between all Christian Churches in strong opposition to Anglo-Catholic exclusiveness; and I may give one example of this catholicity. At the opening of a Board School, the most active of the exclusive clergy declared, ' If there is one name of which I am proud, it is that of Churchman.' The Dean, who followed him, remarked in his gentlest tone, ' I must differ from my friend who has just spoken. If there is one name of which I am proud, it is that of *Christian.*'

2

At the end of three years I married the wife who has been my companion throughout all these years of work for the poor, and has borne the brunt of whatever hardship has attended it. She was the second daughter of Dr. Andrew Davies, J.P., a physician who was, in his later years, managing director of a colliery in Monmouthshire, of which his wife's family were the proprietors. We removed to Wolverhampton, where my hands were filled, not only with church work, but in carrying out, as secretary, a great scheme of chapel-building throughout the circuit, and with organizing Recreative Evening Schools throughout the town, as a lieutenant of Dr. J. B. Paton of Nottingham. In 1887 I was appointed to Cambridge, and of the consequences I must speak later on. Suffice it to say, for the present, that in these five circuits I had a diversified experience, which falls to the lot of few, and that materials for my later career were gained from them all.

Methodism in the Seventies and Early Eighties.

I cannot conclude this section of my Reminiscences without a brief reference to the Wesleyan Methodism of that period. Throughout the seventies and early eighties the chief concern of high politics for leading ministers was little else than the management of Dr. Osborn. To say nothing of other difficulties, Dr. Dallinger's Fernley Lecture was held up in 1880 because he advocated the hypothesis of Evolution. Dr. Osborn was stubborn in his opposition, and the rest discovered that, while the doctrine was probably true, its advocacy at that moment would be inopportune. The selfsame lecture was delivered at Manchester in 1887, and, to use a common expression, no one was a penny the worse.

On a hot July evening in 1881 I met Dr. Pope in Southport, just returned from an arduous week's work in London. He had been engaged in revising the First Catechism, and he said to me, ' I have fought a great battle and won a great victory. You remember the first question and answer of the Catechism, '' What is God? An infinite and eternal Spirit.'' Well, I have got them to alter that, and now it is to be, '' Who is God? Our Father.'' '

I love to think of the great dogmatic teacher of Methodism giving back to its children the simplicity of the gospel. ' But,' he added, ' I have had great trouble with Dr. Osborn : he says God is not their Father! ' While I was in Cardiff, Dr. Osborn, then in his second Presidency, sent for me and urged me to take the appointment at Stuttgart. Cogent reasons prevented me from accepting this proposal; and having explained them, I added that both my judgement and my conscience were against it. Immediately Dr. Osborn replied, ' Speak of your judgement, if you like, but not of your conscience. I hold that, when the Methodist Conference has spoken, no man has a right to have a conscience against it.' From such absolutism happily later generations have been delivered.

III.

FERNLEY LECTURER

MY life has been devoted to the work of the Christian ministry, as I have understood it; and in its course I have been called upon to discharge all the tasks that are involved in such ministry as carried on by the Wesleyan Methodist Church. Yet, subject to this major obligation, my chief activities have been concerned with theological writing and teaching, with the foundation and direction of the Bermondsey Settlement, and with public affairs. In dealing with all these in succession, it is necessary to draw aside the veil and describe certain inward and decisive experiences in regard to them all, which have, I think, both religious and psychological significance. In speaking frankly and fully about these, I will endeavour simply to state what happened, trusting to avoid any suspicion of egotism or of exaggeration. Hitherto I have kept these matters strictly to myself.

To begin with, I must give a brief account of the way in which my call to the ministry came to me. As I have already said, my family, and especially my uncle, had intended that I should enter into business. I had, however, set my heart upon going to the Bar, and had consulted my uncle, Mr. (afterwards Sir) Percy Bunting about it. But in the summer of 1870, when I was sixteen years of age, my uncle and aunt, Mr. and Mrs. William H. Budgett of Bristol, invited me, with my cousin Frank Lidgett, to stay with them at Whitby. On the Sunday morning we all went to an old Wesleyan chapel, where the service was conducted by an old-fashioned Wesleyan minister, whose name, as far as I am aware, I never knew. He took for his text the great passage of Ezekiel (iii. 17-21) beginning, ' Son of man, I have made thee a watchman unto the house of

Israel: therefore hear the word at My mouth, and give them warning from Me.' The sermon in itself was commonplace, but the shaft went home. I left the service with the words ' His blood will I require at the watchman's hand ' ringing in my ears and smiting me to the heart. To my relations I appeared to be completely occupied with the opening phases of the Franco-German War, with *Pickwick,* and with the ordinary pleasures of the seaside. But inwardly a hard though short and decisive struggle was taking place, and before the holiday was over I had irrevocably devoted myself to the work of the ministry. My only hesitation came four years afterwards, when my cousin, who was marked out to join his father in business, and had shown brilliant promise, died of typhoid fever contracted in Italy. My uncle, however, soon relieved my anxiety by generously telling me that the irreparable blow that had come to him should not be allowed to make any difference to my career.

The Guiding Hand.

The same kind of decisive intervention has determined every turning-point of my subsequent course. My earliest subsequent concern had to do with theology. In September 1877 I was taking a short vacation at home. One morning, as I was walking on Blackheath (I can point out the exact spot), there came to me a vivid intimation, ' You have got to write a book upon the Atonement, and afterwards to try to show that Christianity is the final and absolute Religion, taking up into itself all that is true in the rest.' So deep was the impression thus suddenly made upon me, without any previous deliberation, that when I went in the same week to The Leys to report progress to Dr. Moulton, I told him tentatively that I felt something had to be done to restate the doctrine of the Atonement. For years this concern slumbered, except that, when called upon at the end of my probation to read a paper to a ministerial association in Southport, I gave a slight sketch of the subject, which was delivered too hurriedly, through shyness, to make much impression. I made no special study whatever of the doctrine

or of its history. When, later on, the summons came to me to
bury myself, as it seemed, in settlement work at Bermondsey, I
placed theological science among the things that I was called to
renounce. Yet just the opposite happened. Hitherto I had
felt too distrustful of myself to embark upon theological
teaching otherwise than in preaching. But in 1893 the late
Mr. Foot, first lieutenant of Mr. Bradlaugh, delivered an
anti-Christian lecture at the Gladstone Club in Bermondsey.
I felt constrained to answer him, and obtained leave from the
club to give a lecture in reply. From that time onwards I gave
regular courses of public lectures in exposition and defence of
the Christian Religion, with the result that my diffidence and
hesitation were overcome.

In 1894 I attended the Birmingham Conference, and went
one Friday, to hear Dr. George Findlay deliver his Fernley
Lecture in Carr's Lane Chapel. Towards the conclusion he
spoke briefly of the Atonement. Immediately a constraining
influence came upon me, and I bent forward in the pew and
made a first sketch of my book on a scrap of paper. On the
following Monday morning I sought out Dr. Moulton in the
Queen's Hotel, and told him, in a stammering way, that I felt
called to write a book on the Atonement. To my immense
surprise, he said at once, ' Why should you not deliver a
Fernley Lecture on the subject? ' I spent my summer holiday
elaborating my preliminary sketch, and submitted it to him in
the following September, with the result that he arranged with
the Rev. Charles H. Kelly that I should be the Fernley
Lecturer in 1897. From that time onwards my holidays and
every moment that I could snatch from other duties were
devoted to completing my book on *The Spiritual Principle of
the Atonement*, which is now in its seventh edition.

My Fernley Lecture.

I had come to see that as the Fatherhood of God, properly
understood, is the highest, so it is the universal relationship in
which He stands to mankind, however lacking may be the
response of sonship. His Fatherhood embraces and, so to speak,

informs and controls all such consequential relationships as sovereignty, &c. Hence the ways of God with men, including the Atonement, must be capable of explanation in terms of this all-embracing Fatherhood, as made manifest in his Son, our Lord Jesus Christ. This Fatherhood must determine the spiritual principle of the Atonement, at once bringing it into line with the gracious purpose of God and calling into full and redemptive expression the true spiritual life of man.

The book seeks to explain and elaborate this point of view. But all was not plain sailing. A few weeks before the Conference at which the lecture was to be delivered, the proofs were held up by the Methodist Publishing House. It was only when Dr. Moulton (to whom the book was dedicated) and I obtained an interview with Mr. Kelly and Mr. Watkinson at the Book-Room, that we learnt that a reviewer, who had been supplied with advance proofs, had brought a charge of heresy against me, and that, without my knowledge, the proof-sheets had been dispatched to the President, Dr. Randles, at the Irish Conference. Eventually Dr. Randles replied that the lecture did not take sufficient account of Divine Justice and that, if the Fernley Lecture was established to support Methodist doctrines, then this lecture was not entitled to a place in the series. With his usual determination, however, Mr. Kelly, without referring to me, gave orders that the book was to be pressed forward for publication; and I went to the Conference at Leeds not knowing what would happen, save that Dr. Moulton had told me that, if necessary, he would defend the book in the Conference. Without going further into details, I need only add that the lecture was delivered, that Dr. Davison gave it a generous and approving review, and that subsequently Dr. Robertson Nicol bore witness to its orthodoxy in a *British Weekly* leading article. This story has its interest and importance; but I should not have told it had it not been for the sequel. In 1902 Dr. Randles asked me to allow him to nominate me for a theological chair, and one of his latest acts was to get my next book on *The Fatherhood of God* (which sets forth exactly the same view as the Fernley Lecture), placed in the Rylands Library in Manchester. His last communication, saying that he had been successful, reached me only a few days before he died. Of my other books, it is only necessary to say that in them I have sought to fulfil the second part of what I felt in 1877 to be my commission, namely, to endeavour to present the Christian religion as final and absolute, transcending, yet containing all elements of truth in other religions.

I may perhaps be permitted to add one remark of a psychological nature. The late Dr. J. H. Jowett once said to me that I must be possessed of a remarkable subliminal consciousness, and many people have inquired how I have managed to carry through so many and such various activities. My answer to them has been that, whatever has been successful in my speech or writing, has always burst upon me complete in outline, and that twelve years of weekly editorial dictation has given me in later years great rapidity, when at ease, in clothing such attempts in verbal expression. Hence very little time is taken up in preparation.

The Bermondsey Settlement.

It has been necessary to outstrip the course of events in order to give a connected account of my theological work; and I now retrace my steps in order to tell of the way in which the Bermondsey Settlement was founded, and to describe the nature of its activities. I entered upon my ministry at Cambridge with a deep though undefined sense that it was to prove momentous in my career. I went there, as I have already explained, much concerned about the growing separation and consequent estrangement of classes, and with a varied experience of a good many kinds of social enterprise, especially in regard to the advancement of popular education. It was at a time when what was called the Condition of the People problem was coming to occupy the foreground of public attention, when the obligation resting upon the educated classes to share their advantages with the less favoured was coming to be realized, and when various projects for fulfilling this obligation were being set on foot with a truly religious enthusiasm. The University Extension Movement had by that time established itself, owing to the leadership of Professor James Stuart and the little band of pioneers, including Richard Green Moulton, who co-operated with him. Toynbee Hall had been recently established in Whitechapel by the Rev. Samuel Barnett; and his example was followed by the subsequent foundation of the Oxford House in Bethnal Green and of the Women's University Settlement in Southwark. These first Settlements aimed at a great improvement and extension of the ideal of the various College and Public School Missions, which owed their initiation largely to Bishop Thorold. Miss Cons had already successfully transformed the ' Old Vic ' from a low-class theatre and music-hall into the home of great opera and popular science, brought within the reach of the working classes of South London and warmly appreciated by them. What was then called ' The Bitter Cry of Outcast London,' in respect particularly to housing, was beginning to be heard. The Wesleyan Methodist Church had already established the East End Mission under Peter Thompson; and the West Central Mission opened its campaign in the autumn of 1887 under the leadership of Hugh Price Hughes, supported by Mrs. Hughes with her Sisterhood and by Mark Guy Pearse. All these new movements had awakened my deepest sympathy; but I felt that something was wanting in the slogan of the Forward Movement in Methodism that ' God cared not only for souls but for bodies.' I wanted to add ' *minds,*' and also to secure the public recognition of the need of transforming social conditions by the co-operation of all classes and not merely of palliating existing evils by charitable help. I hoped to arouse sympathy with all these ideals among such members of the University as might come under my influence.

Life in Cambridge.

On my arrival in Cambridge Dr. Moulton at once transferred to me the leadership of the University Society Class and the general oversight of the University Wesley Society, which he had hitherto exercised. In this way I was brought immediately into weekly contact with a very brilliant group of University men. Among them were W. P. Workman, who became Fellow of Trinity, and James Hope Moulton, who became Fellow of King's, that autumn; A. C. Dixon, Senior Wrangler in 1886; A. W. Flux and J. D. Michell, Senior Wranglers in 1887; W. E. Brunyate, Second Wrangler in 1888, subsequently Smith's Prize Man and Fellow of Trinity (now Sir William Brunyate, K.C.M.G.); G. T. Walker, Senior Wrangler in 1889 (now Sir Gilbert Walker); Owen Thompson (now K.C.), who distinguished himself in the Classical Tripos of 1889; and A. C. Barber, distinguished in Natural Science. This band was recruited later on by W. J. Brown from Australia, whose early distinction in the Law Tripos has been followed by a series of professorships in Law, by Walter (now the Right Hon. Walter) Runciman, and by McCurdy (now the Right Hon. A. C. McCurdy), who came to the Sunday night meetings as a Primitive Methodist. These are only some of the outstanding names of members of the class and of the Society. I soon began to start Recreative Evening Classes in the town, with the help of certain distinguished University tutors, and joined the Executive of the Charity Organization Society, which was largely under the influence and had the unremitting service of Professor Henry Sidgwick.

In all these ways the train was laid, and only the spark was needed to kindle the flame. It came about as follows. On the last Sunday in November, Temperance Sunday was observed as usual, and on the evening of that day I preached a sermon at Hill's Road Chapel to a large congregation, partly composed of The Leys School, which had then no chapel of its own, and with a fair sprinkling of undergraduates. My text was, ' And whether one member suffereth, all the members suffer with it ' (1 Cor. xii. 26). Deeply moved by my subject, I endeavoured to describe the spiritual, intellectual, and physical conditions which did so much to strengthen the temptations in crowded cities to intemperance, and dealt in a way that has since become familiar with the wholeness of society, and with the spiritual loss sustained by the well-to-do, educated, and leisured from their failure to share their advantages and to co-operate with the industrial classes in remedying these adverse and demoralizing conditions. On the following day I learned from many sources of the deep impression my sermon had made upon the congregation, and especially on the masters and boys of The Leys School. That week I heard what seemed to me to be a clear call. I well remember how on the following Thursday night, as I was returning from a country appointment at the little village of Quy, I stood under a moonlight but stormy sky and vowed to God that I would renounce all other interests and seek to lead a movement to give practical and permanent expression to the sympathy my sermon had been the means of evoking. It seemed to me that I must endeavour to plant a colony, somewhat on the lines of Toynbee Hall, in one of the poorest districts of London, to be carried on in a distinctively evangelical spirit, but with the broadest possible educational and social aims.

Dr. Moulton's Help.

I waited until Christmas, and then laid the scheme with some fear and trembling before Dr. Moulton. He at once warmly welcomed the proposal, and gave me, from that hour to the end of his life, his most generous trust, his wise counsel, and his unstinted support. I felt, however, that I owed it to the Cambridge Circuit to complete my three years' term of ministry before entering upon this new task, should Conference permit. Hence we agreed to take no immediate step, save that in the summer of 1888 I went over to Oxford, at the instance of Dr. Moulton, to consult the Principal of Mansfield College as to the possibility of a joint movement. Dr. Fairbairn promised his co-operation; but withdrew some time afterwards, explaining that he had been appealed to by the Rev. F. W. Newland, then a minister in Canning Town, to help in the establishment of a Settlement there. This Settlement, known as Mansfield House, though its inception was later than that of the Bermondsey Settlement, was opened in the summer of 1891, a few weeks before we got to work in Bermondsey. In the beginning of 1889 meetings of the University Wesley Societies were held at Cambridge and Oxford on successive nights, Dr. Moulton accompanying me to the former and Mr. (afterwards Sir) Percy Bunting to the latter. Resolutions at both meetings were passed supporting the scheme. Later on I visited the principal Wesleyan schools throughout the country (excluding The Leys, which had just started the Leysian Mission), in the hope that they might find in the new Settlement something equivalent to a joint School Mission, one of my main objects being to bring all public and Wesleyan schools to accept the ideals of personal social service in the widest sense.

Meanwhile Dr. Moulton and I went to work to ascertain what part of poorest London was most in need of the establishment of such a Settlement as we proposed. The evidence went to show that Bermondsey was almost unhelped at that time by personal service from outside. ' Here in South-east London,' wrote a young man, ' we have nothing between heaven and hell, the church and the public-house.' Dr. Moulton brought the proposal before both sessions of the Wesleyan Methodist Conference at Sheffield in 1889. Resolutions were passed giving general approval, and appointing a provisional committee to prepare the scheme. The very night that the Representative Session gave its consent, I travelled to London from Sheffield, and bought the site in the midst of the waterside population of Bermondsey upon which the Settlement has been built. Before I left Sheffield I received £500 from the late Mr. T. Morgan Harvey, who became our first Treasurer, and £500 from the late Mr. Mewburn. With the aid of Dr. Moulton I had already secured a Guarantee Fund of £500 a year for three years towards the maintenance of the work when set on foot.

IV.
THE BERMONDSEY SETTLEMENT

I SHALL never forget the experiences of the next two years. The powerful influence of Dr. Moulton had procured official and formal approval of the undertaking, yet there was very little real conviction behind it. Some years later, when the Report of the Settlement was brought before the Conference Dr. Rigg expressed his satisfaction with the success of an enterprise, which, he said, he had felt bound to support at the beginning owing to the advocacy of Dr. Moulton, but which he had believed was foredoomed to failure. This, I think, was the general attitude; and as I travelled over the country raising the all too small Building Fund I often felt like a mendicant, hawking his patent in the hope of its being eventually taken up. Moreover, there were many who supposed that I desired in large measure to substitute social activities pursued in a somewhat secular spirit for the gospel and spirituality. I think this impression was largely dissipated by the publication of my book on the Atonement some years later.

Nor were things better on my first appearance in Bermondsey itself. My reception by the large firms was chilly in the extreme. Nor did the clergy and ministers welcome me much more warmly. They assured me that there was no demand in Bermondsey for such a scheme, and that I should meet with little response. They also seemed nervous lest I should bring financial support from outside to inaugurate a work which would damage their own struggling churches. The difficulty was increased by reason of the fact that the enterprise had to be plunged complete on the neighbourhood instead of springing from small beginnings. The one exception was the late Colonel S. B. Bevington, a man of the highest position in the commercial and public life of Bermondsey, who stood by me from the first and right on to the end of his life. However, I set my teeth and toiled on, with the result that the Committee felt justified in taking a building contract early in 1891, that the foundation stone was laid by the Lord Mayor, Sir Joseph Savory, on July 14, and that the main Settlement building was opened for educational work on January 6, 1892. Owing to lack of funds the building could not be completed until 1898, and the plans of the architect, Mr. Elijah Hoole, were to some extent damaged by the rigid economy that had to be imposed.

Before this time, however, I had come to the conclusion that a Settlement for women must be established side by side with that for men. I had therefore sought the help of the late Miss Alice Barlow of Edgeworth, who at once joined me in taking the responsibility for this additional enterprise, a partnership which lasted, on terms of the most intimate friendship and generous support, till her death in 1919. To her and to Miss Mary Simmons, who was head of the Women's House from January 1893 till 1916, and continued in the work for some years longer, I owe the most grateful thanks for their unfailing comradeship and co-operation. The work of the Women's House began in October 1891 by our undertaking, under the Queen Victoria Jubilee Institute, the District Nursing of Rotherhithe, for which I have been responsible ever since.

Aims of the Settlement.

The main object of the Settlement was to bring a force of educated workers to give help to all the higher interests of the neighbourhood, religious, educational, social, and administrative. Its aims were defined at the outset in the following terms :

' 1. To bring additional force and attractiveness to Christian work.

' 2. To become a centre of social life, where all classes may meet together on equal terms for healthful intercourse and recreation.

' 3. To give facilities for the study of Literature, History, Science, and Art.

' 4. To bring men together to discuss general and special social evils and to seek their remedy.

' 5. To take such part in local administration and philanthropy as may be possible.

' 6. And so to do all this that it shall be perfectly clear that no mere sectarian advantage is sought, but that it shall be possible for all good men to associate themselves with our work.'

It is clear from all that has been said that the Settlement differs considerably in aim and therefore in development from a Mission. A Settlement is or should be a community of social workers who come to a poor neighbourhood to assist by the methods of friendship and co-operation those who are concerned in upholding all that is essential to the well-being of the neighbourhood. Hence freedom and initiative are of its essence. Men and women who come to it must be encouraged to see with their own eyes and to respond with a large measure of independence to the calls that are made upon them. A cut-and-dried programme would be fatal both to the conception and to the development of a Settlement. Its head should not stereotype, but guide and co-ordinate all its activities, encouraging adventure, though tempering it with prudence. Much, therefore, will depend upon the temperament and outlook of the settlers who rally to his banner. Moreover, the mental, moral, and material conditions of the particular neighbourhood that is served by any Settlement may encourage and necessitate certain forms of activity, and equally may hinder or thwart certain other endeavours that may be intrinsically desirable. Hence for more than the ordinary reasons there must needs be a considerable interval between the ideal and the practicable. All this has been true of the Bermondsey Settlement.

Varied Agencies.

Space will not allow me to trace the development of the work of the Bermondsey Settlement from 1892 to the present time. The following list of its existing activities must suffice.

Classification is rather difficult; for while the Trust is for Religious, Educational, and Social purposes, the three objects are interfused in many of our institutions.

First and foremost comes the *Educational Institute*, the number of students annually ranging between 500 and 700. The provision of teaching embraces University Extension Courses, chiefly in History, Literature, and Art; Music, Choral and Orchestral; Elocution, Languages (Latin, Greek, French, German, and Italian); instruction in First Aid and Nursing; Art Needlework; and Gymnastics, as well as Commercial subjects, advanced and elementary. There is no overlapping with other educational institutes, and the work is in many respects different from that of the Evening Institutes maintained by the London County Council. Many auxiliary activities for sport and recreation are associated with the Institute.

Side by side with the Institute is the Boys' Brigade work, with its Old Boys' Club, including in its membership many generations of members of the 62nd Company—before the War the premier Company of London.

The women's work of the Settlement is now for the most part concentrated at the *Alice Barlow House*, so named after my lamented friend, and generously supported by her family. This house is the head-quarters of a very large Working Women's Society, of a School for Mothers numbering about a thousand members, of the Beatrice Club for Girls, the Rydal Club for Boys (carried on by old boys of Rydal School, Colwyn Bay), the Rotherhithe Day Nursery, and many other agencies for helping women, girls, and boys. The local branch of the Metropolitan Association for Befriending Young Servants has its head-quarters there, and is carried on by Settlement workers. The Invalid Kitchens of London have established a branch upon the premises for serving nourishing and tempting meals to the sick poor in their own homes. Some of our women residents live at this House, and others are accommodated in a wing of the main Settlement building.

The predominantly Social Work of the Settlement includes

an Insurance branch, having 3,400 members in the State Approved Society, and 2,000 in a Voluntary Organization.

A Minor Ailments and Dental Centre provides medical and nursing attention to more than a thousand waterside children weekly. The work of the Children's Holiday Fund, and also of the Women's Holiday Fund for the whole of Bermondsey, including Rotherhithe, has for many years been organized from the Settlement. The District Nursing of Rotherhithe in connexion with the Queen Victoria Jubilee Institute has been undertaken ever since 1891; and though there is now a local committee, I remain chairman, the work is organized from the Settlement, and I am ultimately responsible for the finances. Free Legal Advice has been given to the poor by a succession of qualified lawyers, of whom the first was Mr. (now the Right Hon. Sir) Kingsley Wood.

In the field of Local Administration the Settlement has furnished workers throughout the past years to the School Board, the London County Council, the Bermondsey Borough Council, and the Board of Guardians. It has supplied many School Managers and Care Workers to the Schools, as well as helpers to many other agencies of public and private philanthropy. In every one of these spheres our method has been that of co-operation with others on the broadest lines, and our aim has always been constructive and not eleemosynary.

While all these agencies and activities are still being carried on by the Settlement, brief mention should be made of some enterprises which, while now conducted independently, were originally started by the Settlement. First in order of time came the election of women as Poor Law Guardians, a thing which had been undreamt of or frowned upon, in the neighbourhood until the Settlement found the women and carried through the campaign.

The magnificent Heritage Craft Schools for Crippled Children at Chailey in Sussex, of which Mrs. Kimmins was the founder and is still the head, sprang from the Bermondsey Settlement, which, to begin with, was responsible for them. I assisted the

3

late Rev. Brooke Lambert in founding the Association for Befriending Boys (those who were placed out in situations from the Poor Law Schools of London), and since his death I have acted as Chairman of the Executive Committee. Did space suffice much more might be said; but this is simply to show the nature and extent of the direct and indirect activities of the Settlement.

Religious Work and Influence.

The religious work and influence of the Settlement, while a factor in many of its agencies, has been concentrated in classes for church workers and Sunday-school teachers of all denominations, lectures in exposition and defence of the Christian Faith, and, for many years, in carrying on two Wesleyan churches in Rotherhithe, now merged in the South London Mission. In later years my work in all these directions has, I regret to say, been necessarily restricted by my duties as Chairman of the Third London District and by other responsibilities. The balance sheets of the various branches of all this work amount in the aggregate to about £7,000 per annum, a very heavy burden, which has often caused me grave anxiety, though this has been lightened in recent years by several munificent contributions, which came at a time of great difficulty, unexpectedly and unsought by me.

One or two features of special interest must be mentioned. Our principal Girls' Club is the Beatrice Club, which occupies the Beatrice Hall of the Alice Barlow House. Its foundation was as follows. In 1893 my colleague, Miss Simmons, was preparing to start our first Girls' Club, but was doubtful of success. At that time I was in constant touch with Beatrice Dunkin, a very brave and saintly girl, whom I had first met at Meldreth, near Cambridge, who had suffered for years from an excruciating spinal complaint, and whom I had, through the assistance of Mrs. (afterwards Lady) Bunting, got placed in a Home at Hendon among convalescent patients. Beatrice took the greatest interest in the foundation and work of the Settlement, and used to send to me, as Chairman of the

Rotherhithe Infirmary, parcels of scent bags made by her in the intervals of long and constant suffering. One day I received a letter from her in which she complained sadly of the uselessness of her life. I was able to send her word that very day that she had started a Girls' Club as successfully as if she had been running about the streets of Rotherhithe. It came to pass in this wise. One of the convalescent patients was employed at Messrs. Peek, Frean & Co's. While at Hendon, Beatrice had interested her in the work of the Settlement, and had made her promise, when leaving, to get into immediate touch with Miss Simmons. She did so, and on learning about the proposed club set herself to work, and brought nearly a hundred girls from the factory and the neighbourhood to join on the opening night.

That club has had a splendid history. A few years ago I met a lady who is now J.P., Mayor of a Metropolitan Borough, Ex-Chairman of a Board of Guardians, and on both the Council and Executive of the National Food Council. She was one of the original members of the Beatrice Club, and she told me that she owed all her success in life to the Settlement.

Distinguished Residents.

Many other cases could be mentioned. Some Settlement students have been prepared for the ministry of various Churches; one holds a good post in the Indian Civil Service, having been coached by one of our residents, Mr. (now Sir) Richard Hopkins, K.C.B., head of Somerset House. The leader of the local Conservative Party, and the very able agent, for many years, of the local Liberal Party, received their training at the Settlement; while the local Labour Party, now in the ascendant, owes its rise and success to Dr. Alfred Salter, M.P., an old Settlement resident; while Mrs. Salter (herself one of our residents before her marriage) has been Mayor of Bermondsey, the first woman Mayor in London.

A word must be said about our Music, because not only has our Choral and Orchestral Union been highly successful, but we have carried out for years, with the assistance of the London County Council, a great scheme for bringing together once or twice a year a choir of at least 600 school children—some of them from the poorest schools—to sing in great oratorios such as the ' The Messiah,' ' The Elijah,' &c. The Marquess of Crewe, K.G., when Chairman of the London County Council, and the Right Hon. H. A. L. Fisher, when President of the Board of Education, told me that they had never heard anything like it in their lives.

I wish I could speak of many of the residents of the Settlement; but space will not allow of this. Some of them have attained great distinction, as, for example, Mr. (now Sir) William Brunyate, K.C.M.G., late Legal and for some time also Financial Adviser to the Khedive's Government; H. Boyd Carpenter, who started our Picture Exhibitions, and subsequently took charge of Education in Egypt; Dr. C. W. Kimmins, who has recently retired from the Chief Inspectorship of Schools under the London County Council; Dr. John E. Borland, our Musical Director, who became Musical Adviser to the Schools of London under the London County Council; and Sir Richard Hopkins, who has just been mentioned. Dr. Lofthouse entered the ministry from the Settlement, and has carried his social enthusiasm with him into all the works of scholarship in which he has been distinguished. And many more are held by me in grateful memory. One other I must mention. My only son, John Cuthbert Lidgett, B.A., LL.B., had been my right hand, giving help in Boys' work, in teaching Latin and Greek, in insurance administration, and in giving legal advice. He fell in battle on Palm Sunday, March 24, 1918, while covering the withdrawal of his battalion in the great German offensive. His commanding officer on that day wrote to me that ' he could not have died a braver or a nobler death.'

The rest of these Reminiscences will be taken up with my more strictly public life, of which the Bermondsey Settlement has been the centre and the starting-point.

V.

GUARDIAN AND SCHOOL BOARD MEMBER

I T has already been stated that one of the declared objects of the Bermondsey Settlement from the outset was ' to take such part in local administration and philanthropy as may be possible.' The opportunity soon came to me to put this into practice. The, at that time, annual election of Poor Law Guardians came in the spring of 1892, within three months of the opening of the Settlement. These elections, like all the rest, were conducted mainly upon party political lines. The local Progressive Party invited me to become a candidate for the parish of Bermondsey, and their declared programme was more entirely in accordance with my principles and aims than any other. Yet this involved my becoming to a considerable extent committed to political action, which was indeed my only way of entrance into public life. Before coming to a decision I took counsel with Dr. Moulton, laying before him the risks which I foresaw would attend this course. His immediate and sympathetic answer was, ' Mr. Lidgett, we sent you to Bermondsey to take risks.' Assured by this judgement, I consented to stand, and was returned high up on the list of successful candidates. It may be of interest to add that at that time a considerable property qualification was demanded as a condition of being a Poor Law Guardian, and that only occupiers were electors. The voting was open—sheets being handed out and collected from door to door by the Relieving Officers. This method, which provided opportunities far various irregularities, was altered by Mr. H. H. Fowler (afterwards Viscount Wolverhampton) when he was President of the Local Government Board.

Board of Guardians.

I threw myself energetically into this new work in order to meet its exacting demands. I became at once Chairman of the Committee of one of our Workhouses, and at the end of that year entered upon the chairmanship of the Rotherhithe Infirmary Committee, which was responsible for the care of more than six hundred patients. This post I held till my engagements at the London County Council and as President of the National Council of Evangelical Free Churches brought my Guardianship to an end in 1906. Once previously I had resigned, but at the urgent instance of the Board had returned as a co-opted member in order that my work at the Infirmary might be continued. In 1894 I secured the election of two lady guardians, of whom my colleague, Miss Mary Simmons, was one. I also served on the Board of the South Metropolitan District Schools at Sutton, one of the much maligned 'Barrack' Schools. In that capacity, and utilizing also my position on the London School Board, I organized an exhibition of the work of the Poor Law Schools of London, which was held in 1900 and again in 1901, and did a good deal to correct the undue depreciation, then current, of the educational work of these schools. The former of these two exhibitions was graciously opened by the present King and Queen, then the Duke and Duchess of Cornwall and York. The whole of the work of organizing these Exhibitions was carried out by the Settlement.

On one occasion I was invited to become a candidate for the chairmanship of the Board of Guardians; but I declined, on the ground that it was the year of the Quinquennial Valuation, and that, as the Chairman of the Board was at that time the *ex-officio* Chairman of the Valuation Committee, it might shake the confidence of the owners of property if this responsibility were assumed by a minister of religion. Subsequently I have on two occasions been invited to become a candidate for the Mayoralty of Bermondsey, although I have never been a member of the Borough Council. On the first occasion I consented, but was defeated owing to the action, or rather inaction, of the

Labour Party. On the second occasion, when my election would have been certain, the pressure of other duties compelled me to decline the honour.

The London School Board.

In the autumn of 1897 a more important call came to me. The Triennial School Board Election was held on November 27 of that year; and the Rev. J. C. Carlile, one of the members of the Southwark Division—which included Bermondsey and Rotherhithe—was retiring, owing to his acceptance of a Church in Folkestone. The cinders of what was known as the Circular Controversy were still hot. This Circular, issued in 1893 by the Rev. J. W. Diggle (the Chairman of the Board) largely at the instance of Mr. Athelstan Riley, had made inquiry into and sought assurance in regard to the dogmatic beliefs of the teachers in the London Board Schools. The uproar and upheaval caused by the controversy that ensued were largely responsible for the decision of the majority of the Bermondsey Progressive Association to fight the election on the platform of Secular Education. The minority, which was composed of members of Christian Churches, came to me and besought me to allow myself to be nominated as candidate on the basis of maintaining biblical instruction and religious influence in the schools. After securing the approval of Dr. Moulton and my treasurer, the late Mr. T. Morgan Harvey, and with the consent of the Committee of the Settlement, I accepted the invitation, and was adopted by a majority of the Association. The Secularist section struck at once; and as this section included the officials of the Association, the use of their lists of voters, &c., was refused to me. So I set to work, with the help of Miss Simmons, and of the late Mr. Henry Hall, a fine-spirited United Free Methodist, and formed an Election Committee of my own, arranged a canvass of the whole of Bermondsey and Rotherhithe, and carried on a platform campaign for a month, with the result that, owing to the cumulative vote, I headed the poll by several thousand votes.

That election gave the Progressives a large majority; and as the next and last election in 1900 again furnished a majority, the

Party was in power until the School Board gave place to the London County Council owing to the London Education Act of 1903. The Party at once selected Lord Reay, a man of high Christian character, of extensive administrative experience in India, and of genuine educational enthusiasm, as Chairman of the Board, a position which he occupied to general satisfaction as long as the School Board lasted. The Leader was the Hon. E. Lyulph Stanley, afterwards Lord Sheffield and Lord Stanley of Alderley, whose unrivalled ability and services to elementary education made him the only possible leader. He was a most remarkable man. His enthusiasm burned at white heat, his knowledge extended even to the building-plan and the exact situation of every Board School in London, while his courage and determination brooked no obstacles in the path of advance, whether they were found on the Board itself or in Whitehall. His marvellous knowledge, swift comprehension and decision, and defiance of difficulties would have been still more effective had it not been for his impetuosity and impatience. During the latest years of the Board it became my duty, as Chief Whip of the Party, to seek to moderate these drawbacks in counsel and to counteract their effects on his party and on the Board.

Formative Years.

Those were great years, and but for the work that was done in them I do not know how it would have stood subsequently with the Elementary Education of London. The primary task was to secure that a school place was promptly provided for every child of school age, both by the enlargement, where necessary, of existing schools and the erection of new ones to meet the needs of the new and rapidly growing suburban populations. This was at that time a controversial task, for scarcely any enlargement or extension could be undertaken without overcoming the opposition of clergy interested in Voluntary Schools supported by ratepayers concerned at the rise of the Education Rate. Then came the improvement of school buildings, both in the planning of new schools, and in providing Assembly Halls in old ones, as well as in partitioning and reducing the size of class-rooms in order to make effective teaching possible and to lighten the strain upon the teachers.

Side by side with the policy of improvement of buildings went the successful effort to raise the qualifications of the teaching staff and to extend the range of elementary education in all directions, including the teaching of French, physical science, music, and drawing and gymnastics. Nor were the interests of domestic and manual instruction neglected. Centres for the teaching of cookery, laundry, and housewifery were multiplied for girls, and woodwork and metalwork centres for boys. Care was given to the provision of centres for mentally and physically defective children. In short, those six fruitful years transformed the conditions of elementary education throughout London and raised the standard for all future time.

The Cockerton Judgement.

This beneficial work was rudely, though only temporarily, interfered with in 1901 by the celebrated Cockerton Judgement. An opposition composed of clerics and ratepayers, as well as of middle-class people, who complained that the rates were being used to enable the children of the industrial classes to compete for employment with their own expensively educated sons, directed the attention of the auditor to certain items of expenditure by the School Board, and these items were disallowed. A lawsuit followed, and the judgement, although the Judges cautiously refused to set fixed limits to the improvement of Elementary Education as the capacity of the children improved, went against the School Board. But at once a storm arose. Certain of the northern School Boards had adopted a policy of higher Elementary Education, and the Tory Democrats who held seats in these constituencies stood to lose them if matters were allowed to remain as the Judgement left them. Incidentally the Wesleyan Schools were hard hit; for they were maintained in being only through the provision of such advanced education as met the needs of small tradesmen and artisans, with the special grants for teaching more advanced subjects that had in recent years been available. Thus the conflict brought me into active co-operation with **Dr. Rigg**, with whom my relations had been severely strained shortly before owing to his displeasure at certain features of the London Progressive policy in regard to the Denominational Training Colleges. The result was that Sir John Gorst, Vice-President of the Council (which administered education previously to the creation of the present Board of Education), was compelled to regularize the position by giving special grants to so-called Higher Elementary Schools, which drew scholars from the surrounding ordinary schools, and which have by this time been superseded by the Central Schools, which stand, with a bias either industrial or commercial, between the ordinary Elementary and the Secondary Schools.

During the closing years of the School Board the general educational administration was in the hands of Mr. (then Lord) Stanley, Mr. (now Professor) Graham Wallas, Chairman of the School Management Committee, and myself, as Vice-Chairman of that Committee, Chief Whip, and Chairman of the Special Subjects Sub-Committee (which dealt with the more advanced education). In this last post I had Mr. William Bridgeman (now the First Lord of the Admiralty, and recently Home Secretary) as my lieutenant in charge of physical education. Dr. (now the Right Hon.) T. J. Macnamara was in charge of School Accommodation and Attendance, and, on his election to Parliament, was a spokesman of the Board in the House of Commons; while the late Rev. Stewart D. Headlam was carrying out the far-reaching policy of Evening Continuation Schools with which his name will be for ever connected. The Chairman of the Finance Committee was the late Sir Charles Elliott, a retired Indian administrator, a deeply religious man, and a Moderate of independent mind and wider outlook than the rest. In those years Party considerations were never allowed to interfere with opportunities for service on the Board, where men and women came to the work with goodwill and devotion to the cause of the children.

VI.
THE GREAT EDUCATION CONTROVERSY

IT was during these years of exacting work upon the London School Board that I came to play an increasing part in the Connexional affairs of Wesleyan Methodism. I had been for some years a member of various Committees, including the Home Mission Committee and the Education Committee. But I had not been greatly concerned in denominational administration. In 1896, however, it became clear that the Conservative Government would be likely to undertake legislation on the Education question. Indeed, they had already made an unsuccessful attempt to do so. The Conference, therefore, of that year, which was held in Liverpool, appointed a Special Committee to deal with the subject. It so happened that at the Conference I made a successful speech in response to a sudden challenge upon the question of the relation of the Church to Recreation, an issue that was raised in regard to what are called Institutional Churches. So it came about that I was appointed Convener of this Special Education Committee, and was at once brought into intimate relations with all the protagonists in the early stages of the controversy. In particular, I received the confidences—always frank and sometimes amusing—both of Dr. Rigg and of Hugh Price Hughes.

The 1902 Education Controversy.

Then in 1897 the Rev. C. H. Kelly secured my appointment on the Executive Committee of the newly-formed National Council of Evangelical Free Churches, and soon after I became Secretary of its Education Committee, while in 1899, on Mr. Kelly's retirement from the office, I was appointed Ministerial Secretary of the Committee of Privileges, with Mr. (afterwards

Sir) Percy Bunting as my Lay colleague. Hence, in addition to my position on the London School Board, I was charged with other Educational responsibilities when the introduction of Mr. Balfour's Education Bill in 1902 brought about the great storm of Educational controversy. The primary cause of that measure was, of course, the financial plight of the Voluntary—now the Non-provided—Schools, which could not approach the new standards set up by the School Boards, and found it impossible to maintain even their existing unsatisfactory level, owing to the decline of enthusiasm in the cause and the consequent falling off of subscriptions. Other influences were at work.

In view of the recent development of local government through the creation of County, District, and Parish Councils, growing objection was taken to the existence of *ad hoc* bodies, particularly the School Boards, with their independent power to call upon the rates and the steady increase of their demands. It was thought that their abolition and the transfer of their duties to the ordinary Municipal Authorities would successfully temper onesided Educational enthusiasm and extravagance by the balanced judgement and prudence of bodies charged with the control of all local concerns. Then the Municipal Authorities had already been charged with the administration of Technical Education, maintained by the so-called ' Whisky money,' and the development of Secondary Education was coming to be seen as needing Municipal support and control. In face of all these factors of opposition, the position of the School Boards was weakened owing to the fact that they had never become universal, and that local oppositions to their establishment were increasingly active. So it came about that the Voluntary Schools were to be maintained out of the rates, that the School Boards were to be abolished, and that the control and maintenance of all forms of Education, with a view to their ' co-ordination,' was henceforth to be vested in the Councils, with the one great exception that their control of the Voluntary Schools was incomplete, and that the denominational character of these Schools was to be preserved both in the appointment of teachers and in the nature of the religious instruction to be given. Both the theoretic and the practical grievances of this imperfect control and these intrenched privileges were increased by the fact that as an investigation made by the Committee of Privileges, at the instance and expense of Mr. (now Sir Robert) Perks, showed, there were 8,000 'single school areas' in England and Wales, where Elementary Education was entirely in the hands of the Established Church.

Nonconformity in Revolt.

Thus it came about that practically the whole of Nonconformity was in revolt, and that a fighting alliance between the National Free Church Council, the champions of the School Boards, and the Liberal Party was brought about. Incidentally the conflict had the damaging result that the National Free Church Council, which was originated not merely for the maintenance and furtherance of Free Church principles and ideals but as a practical instalment of that larger Reunion to which its founders had looked forward, became the protagonist in an embittered strife with the Anglican and Roman Catholic Churches and immersed in a political campaign, which, of necessity, assumed the form of a close alliance with one particular Party,—the Liberal,—in the State.

At the outset, a great meeting of protest was held in St. James's Hall, and a Deputation to Mr. Balfour was appointed. The leading spokesman of this Deputation was the Principal of Mansfield College, Dr. A. M. Fairbairn. With the dour determination of a Scotsman, and the ardour so often shown by men who emerge from academic seclusion to take part in public affairs, he ended his speech by the declaration, 'We will not submit.' This declaration of war struck the key-note and trumpet-call to the Passive Resistance Movement. The impassioned fervour of Dr. Clifford and his slogan, 'Rome upon the rates,' led to its organization during the summer and autumn of 1902. Both Dr. Fairbairn and Dr. Clifford were confident that this declaration and display of conscientious and determined opposition would lead to the withdrawal of the Bill. They underrated both the pertinacity of Mr. Balfour and the cohesion of the Conservative forces in Parliament.

The Wesleyan Conference, which met that year in Manchester under the Presidency of Dr. J. Shaw Banks, joined in the protest against the Bill, though, owing to its existing interests in denominational Education, the protest was more measured and not unanimous. Hence the subject came to be remitted to a joint meeting of the Extraordinary Committee of Privileges and the Education Committee, which met to consider the situation early in 1903. As Ministerial Secretary of the Committee of Privileges I had the chief responsibility for the arrangements and for dealing with the decisions of the meeting.

Free Church Council and Passive Resistance.

During the preceding autumn, however, I had been busily engaged upon the subject, and particularly in a successful endeavour to keep the National Free Church Council from identifying itself with the Passive Resistance Movement. I felt strongly that the distinction between aid from the Rates and aid from the Taxes—though real—was too fine, that the precedent that would be set was too dangerous, and that the result would be too divisive for the National Free Church Council to take part in it. Having rallied strong Wesleyan and Presbyterian support, I made such representations to the Executive Committee of the Council as led Dr. Clifford frankly, though reluctantly, to see that the situation was impossible, and as the result he and his supporters immediately formed the National Passive Resistance Committee on lines of entire independence of the National Free Church Council.

The Education Bill of 1902 passed into law, and was succeeded by the Education Bill for London, which occupied part of the session of 1903. The reason why London was dealt with in a separate measure was that the division of its general local government between the County Council, the City Corporation, and the twenty-eight established Borough Councils raised certain administrative problems special to itself. The general principles of the London Bill were the same as those of the Act of 1902, but the Bill, in its first form, conferred such responsibilities upon the Borough Councils as would have effectually destroyed the unity and coherence of Education in London. Hence, in addition to the ordinary Parliamentary opposition, personal explanations had to be given and personal influences used in all the quarters where the main responsibility for the Bill rested. In making these representations Lord Reay, Sir Charles Elliott, Mr. Bridgeman and I all took an active part. As the result an amended Bill was substituted, which gave the London County Council practically complete control of all forms of Education in the County, and thus an immense educational disaster was averted.

Death of Hugh Price Hughes.

While this great controversy was in process Wesleyan Methodism sustained a terrible loss in the sudden and unexpected death of Hugh Price Hughes. Before I end this narrative I shall have something more to say about him and the great contests in which he engaged, particularly with Dr. Rigg. For the moment I will content myself with speaking of the shock that came to me through his death and of its effect upon my subsequent career. I had been with him at Zion College a few hours before he passed away, to hear an address upon St. Francis of Assisi given by M. Paul Sabatier. My book on *The Fatherhood of God in Christian Truth and Life* had just appeared, and Mr. Hughes had been reading it for review in *The Methodist Times*. He stopped, as he came into the meeting, to speak about it and to tell me that he had preached upon the book at St. James's Hall the night before. Subsequently Mrs. Hughes lent me the notes of this sermon, and I heard of his conversation with the Sisters of the West London Mission over the tea-table before he preached it. The fatal seizure came to him, as will be remembered, on his way home from that meeting. It is easy, therefore, to imagine my consternation, when, on entering the dining hall of the Settlement for breakfast the next morning, I was met by the announcement ' Hugh Price Hughes is dead.' I actually leapt in the air, and shut myself up for the whole of that morning in sorrow and thought. Not only was I overwhelmed by the loss that had come, particularly to Methodism, as well as to the Churches and the nation, but I felt that a crisis had arisen in my own career.

Wesleyan Methodism and National Education.

As I have already described, my interest at the time had been absorbed and my energies were fully taxed with the concerns of the Bermondsey Settlement, with the work of the London School Board, with the Education controversy and with theological writing. I had not felt, hitherto, any deep sense of responsibility in regard to ecclesiastical matters, either denominational or general, but had been content to follow, with reservations, the lead of Mr. Hughes. Now I felt that the situation was entirely altered, and that I was under an obligation to play my part in the general life and policy of the Church, as well as in special concerns. In particular, and for the time being, this meant for me increased responsibility in helping to shape the policy of Wesleyan Methodism in regard to National Education, and this duty I sought to discharge at the united meeting of the Committee of Privileges with the Education Committee, to which I have already referred, and during the months that intervened between that meeting and the Conference of 1903. My position was not altogether easy, for while strongly opposed to the Balfour legislation on the grounds I have already explained, yet my hereditary association with denominational Education made me respect both the motives and the feelings of those who supported it.

In pursuance of the policy laid down by the Joint Committee I was requested, at a private consultation, to propose the series of Education Resolutions at the Conference, which were to be seconded by Mr. (now Sir Robert) Perks. Meanwhile I had been nominated to the Presidency of the Metropolitan Federation of Free Churches, and, in that capacity and in the absence abroad of the then President, Dr. J. Monro Gibson, I presided over a great meeting of protest against the London Education Bill that was held, just before the

Conference, at the Albert Hall. In regard to this meeting, by the way, an interesting incident may be recalled. The late Sir Robert Morant, who was generally believed to have had great influence in shaping the Government policy, had applied to me for a ticket to attend the meeting, and he sat by my wife in a box, smiling pleasantly while Mr. Perks denounced his maleficent activity to the vast audience. As I journeyed to the Conference at Camborne, filled with anxiety about the impending issue and my own responsibility in regard to it, I was visited by the influence that has again and again come to me at the turning-points of my life. The consequence was that when I rose in the Conference to make my speech I was lifted out of myself, and my speech made an immense impression upon the audience. Whatever may have been the merits of my argument, one thing is quite certain. That speech made me, first of all, President of the National Council of Evangelical Free Churches in 1906, and then President of the Conference in 1908. It opened an altogether new chapter in my public life.

VII.

LONDON COUNTY COUNCIL LABOURS

B EFORE continuing the narrative, I may perhaps be
permitted to make a few observations about the period
of Wesleyan Methodist history that came to an end
with the death of Hugh Price Hughes. That period had been
filled by controversies in which Dr. Rigg and he had been
the ministerial protagonists. Both these remarkable men had
their life-work fixed by the conditions and influences
that prevailed in their early life. The clash between
them was determined by these contrasted conditions and
influences, though it was made more violent by personal
qualities, on both sides, that coloured pertinacity and
pugnacity with prejudice and intense feeling. Dr. Rigg was
a Constitutionalist, not only by the original bent of his mind,
but by the conditions of his early ministry. The breaches and
secessions of Methodism, the Tractarian Movement, and the rise
of Anglo-Catholicism, together with the inevitable reactions
towards the ' Latitudinarianism ' which he feared, constrained
Dr. Rigg, both in teaching and in practical effort, to define and
differentiate Wesleyan Methodism, as he conceived its genius
and organization, in contradistinction, alike to the other
Methodist bodies, to the High Church Movement, and to Dissent.
He had recognized the necessity of admitting laymen to
Conference, and had borne a great part in bringing about that
reform. But after this had been successfully accomplished, all
his energies were devoted to administering Wesleyan Methodism
and maintaining intact those features of its *ethos* and
organization which justified, for him, its distinctive and separate
existence. He embodied and gave expression to the tendencies
of a generation, which led a superintendent of mine in the early

eighties to complain of my miscellaneous activities on the ground
that ' Conference sent me here, not to do aggressive work, but to
conserve Methodism,' and in later years caused a worthy minister
to inquire of me, concerning my work on the School Board,
' What does Methodism get out of all this? ' In a new age,
justice should still be done to the statesmanship and vigilance
with which Dr. Rigg maintained the consistency and coherence
of the Wesleyan Methodist Constitution. It is not too much to
say that even the Constitution under which Methodist Union
will be effected will owe much to his life-work. His influence
would have been much greater had it not been for his impatience,
which sometimes caused him to brush aside facts and to be
impatient of weighty reasons. Like many masterful personalities, he was inclined somewhat to resent independence of
thought and action, while being unduly influenced by inferior
men who made a point of ' playing up ' to him.

Hugh Price Hughes' Greatness.

The greatness of Hugh Price Hughes, on the other
hand, lay in the swift and penetrating intuitions by which
he sensed the coming time, with the demands it was already
making and would increasingly make upon the Church. For
him fearless and aggressive evangelism, the uncompromising
and audacious application of Christian principles to public
affairs and humanitarian claims, were the prime qualities
demanded of the Church. In face of the supreme challenge and
commission given to the Church to be even more the instrument
than the embodiment of the Kingdom of God, the cause of
Reunion loomed large before him, and he became not merely
weary, but intolerant, of the differences that have caused the
divisions of Catholic and Evangelical Christendom. He saw that
the age of triumphant democracy had come for both Church and
State, and felt that democracy needed, above all, dauntless and
inspiring leadership. In his case, as well as in that of his great
opponent, certain personal qualities—his impetuosity and
impatience, together with his frequent neglect of details and
rough handling of opponents in the pursuit of his main

objectives—contributed to intensify strife. Happily these antagonisms were ended from the time of his Presidency in 1898, and the Wesleyan Methodist structure, which we owe so largely to Dr. Rigg, has been animated by the spirit that breathed through Hugh Price Hughes. With the passing of Hughes and the waning of Dr. Rigg came the ascendency of Dr. Henry J. Pope in the councils of Wesleyan Methodism, of which more must be said later on.

L.C.C. the Education Authority.

But to resume my narrative. The London School Board passed out of existence at the end of April 1904. All the survivors of previous Boards were invited to be present at its last meeting. So it happened that Mr. John B. Ingle, a Wesleyan Methodist representative of Southwark on the first School Board, and I, one of the members for Southwark on the last, met to close its account and commemorate its history.

On May 1, 1904, the London County Council became the Education Authority for London, charged, not only to take over the work of the School Board, but also with the care of Secondary and Technical Education, as well as with the oversight and maintenance of the Non-provided Schools. The transition was in many ways difficult. A considerable section of the London County Council, including its then leader, Mr. (afterwards the Right Honourable) T. McKinnon Wood, had been opposed to the imposition of these new duties upon the Council. The Council as a whole was unversed in educational administration, save in respect of the very limited operations of the Technical Education Board. Moreover, the majority were somewhat prejudiced against the methods of the School Board—a prejudice which was manifested by their appointment of Sir William Richmond, R.A., to a vacant Aldermanship in preference to Lord Stanley, thus dispensing with the services of the latter in taking over the new work. But the Council co-opted six members of the School Board as members of the Education Committee for the two initial years, and I was one of these. Previously the arrangements for the transfer were handed over to a joint committee, of which Sir

William Collins, K.C.V.O., Mr. (now the Right Hon. Sir)
Willoughby H. Dickinson, and Mr. (now the Right Hon.) Sidney
Webb were the most influential members on the Council side;
Mr. Graham Wallas and I on that of the School Board. It was
an arduous task, but all was ready by the appointed day.
The line of action adopted by the Council was to appoint certain
of its old members to the chairs of the new Education Committee
and its Sub-Committees, having for their lieutenants ex-members
of the School Board as Vice-Chairmen. So it came to pass that I
became Vice-Chairman of the Elementary Education Committee,
Mr. (now the Right Hon. Sir) Edwin Cornwall being the
Chairman. In the following March Mr. Cornwall became
Chairman of the Council, and I succeeded him as Chairman of
the Elementary Education Committee during the remaining two
years of Progressive ascendency upon the Council.

At the outset a very difficult task was assigned to me. I was
appointed Chairman of the Section which fixed the numbers and
qualifications of the Teaching Staff of all the Non-provided
Schools, Anglican and Roman Catholic, throughout London. The
work was lengthy and laborious; for consideration had to be
given, not only to the size, but to the organization and buildings
of each school. It was made the more anxious by reason of the
suspicion and persistence of the two representatives of the
National Schools, the late Mr. John Taylor and Miss Susan
Lawrence, now a very active member of the Labour Party, but
then a perfervid Conservative and supporter of the Non-provided
Schools. Eventually, however, the examination of various types
and sizes of schools enabled us to fix upon certain principles of
staffing, and the work was finished on lines that proved
permanent, save for such changes as have been brought about by
the general advance of Elementary Education and the progress
of the schools. The staffing of the schools was carried on side
by side with the work of another Section, which inspected the
buildings of these schools and imposed plans of structural
improvements upon the denominational managers, closing a small
minority of the schools, where such improvement was impossible.

Subsequently, as Chairman of the Elementary Schools Sub-Committee, I presided over the Section that settled the policy and planned the distribution of the Central Schools, which, owing to the Scholarship Scheme, have proved such a splendid development of higher Elementary Education in London.

Fighting for Council Schools.

It was no easy matter to get the County Council into the full swing of its new duties as the Education Authority for London. The late Lord Welby, the distinguished Chairman of the Finance Committee, was taken aback when, almost at once, a first batch of Council Secondary Schools, and then a fresh batch of Elementary Schools came up for Capital and then for Maintenance Expenditure. The work was held up while an investigation into the cost of buildings was conducted, which led to the complete justification of the standard of buildings that had been set up by the School Board. But Lord Welby was simply aghast when, after a short interval, a second batch of Elementary Schools was required in order to keep pace with the growth of London, so that a school place might be promptly provided for every child of school age. The discovery that no limit short of this and no delay in accomplishing it could be tolerated simply shocked the financiers, who were inexperienced in Educational administration. While this work of educating the educators was proceeding, Mr. McKinnon Wood did me the honour of securing my election as an Alderman in 1905, so that my services might be continued after the two years of temporary co-optation on the Education Committee should have ended, and in order that my voice on Educational questions might be heard in the Council itself. For this purpose he obtained the resignation of Sir William Richmond, who had found administrative work uncongenial and had taken little part in it. So I succeeded to the unexpired term of his Aldermanship, which lasted till March 1910.

The L.C.C. Election of 1907 brought about the momentous defeat of the Progressive Party, which had held power from the start of the Council in 1889; and the Moderates, now the

Municipal Reformers, gained the majority, which they have held ever since. That defeat was due to many causes. In part, it was brought about because the Conservative Party rallied in full strength to the attack. Its forces were strengthened and its financial resources increased by the support of many vested interests, which revolted against municipal enterprise and were alarmed, in particular, by the proposal to establish municipal control of the generation and distribution of electricity. This policy, had it been adopted, would have saved London from a chaos of divergent, ineffective, and wasteful systems of supply, from which the recently established Electricity Authority is now called upon to extricate London at great cost and in face of almost insuperable obstacles. Charges of extravagance were hurled against every department of the Council's administrations: Trams, Works, Improvements, and, last of all, the Steamboats, which, owing to certain intrinsic difficulties, but most of all to a succession of wet and stormy summers, had resulted in a financial loss, which those Londoners who were remote from the River, refused to share. Educational administration added to the discontent, for many of the ratepayers grudged its cost, while those who were influenced by the clergy complained that the Council had been stingy in its support and exacting in its requirements of the Non-provided Schools. Above all, the attack was assisted by a ceaseless, ill-informed, and unscrupulous press campaign, the virulence of which has never been approached in any election since, whether parliamentary or municipal. In particular, *The Standard* launched charges on the eve of the election, and afterwards, when they had taken effect, withdrew them and apologized, in face of the libel action which had been set on foot.

So the process of educating the educators had to be undertaken, once more, in the Council 1907-1910. I shall never forget the first meeting. Only partially recovered from a severe attack of gastric influenza, and hardly able to stand, I had to defend such proposals of the defunct Education Committee as concerned Elementary Education and appeared on the Agenda of the new

Council. Every one of them was referred back for further
consideration. ' What need was there to teach French in
Elementary Schools? ' for example. What need apparently of
anything save instruction in the three R's? Slowly, however,
but surely, and with much travail, the situation and the work
vindicated themselves. On examination, the charges vanished
into thin air. Certain enterprises were abandoned; in the case
of certain others, the slogan ' Go slow! ' prevailed for a time.
Yet the main fabric of administration, reared by the Progressives,
survived the shock and stood the most persistent investigation.
The genius of the Council and the exigencies of London, enforced
by the minority, transformed the bulk of the Moderates into
Municipal Reformers. A new race of administrators sprang up,
and banished such of the old reactionaries as remained to the
back benches. In particular, the claims of Education slowly but
steadily awakened conviction and good-will. With the war, the
need of Municipal Housing, which had been disputed, came home
to the conscience of the Council. Those who passed through the
sad and stormy days of 1907 can best appreciate the welcome
change that has come about. The history of the past twenty
years on the Council has given an additional proof that
eventually ' Wisdom is justified of her children.'

VIII.

FREE CHURCH COUNCIL AND EDUCATION

IN March 1906 I became President of the National Council of Evangelical Free Churches. In many respects this was the most arduous year of my life; for, in addition to the important Educational work I have just described and the care of the Bermondsey Settlement, I was preaching twice every Sunday to the same congregation, and was using every spare moment for completing my book on *The Christian Religion: its Meaning and Proof*. In the course of that twelve months I held nearly fifty Day Conventions in all parts of the country. The programme each day was exceedingly heavy; for it began with an address to the ministers and church workers of the district, followed by a speech at the public luncheon. Then I conducted a public service and preached in the afternoon, talked at a Tea-Table Conference, and spoke for an hour, chiefly on the spiritual unity of the Church and on the Education question, at night. This was generally followed by a supper with the ministers of the neighbourhood and an early start the next morning.

Yet behind the scenes I had to bear much graver and more anxious responsibilities. Sir Henry Campbell-Bannerman had become Prime Minister and formed his Government in the preceding December, and the General Election of January 1906 had given him an immense majority, which included something like 200 Free Churchmen. The Government was pledged to bring in an Education Bill to establish complete popular control over all forms of Education as its first legislative measure. Mr. Birrell was President of the Board of Education, and the Cabinet at once appointed a Sub-Committee to prepare the Bill. Mr. Lloyd George was a member of this Sub-Committee, and was deputed to keep in special touch with certain Free Church leaders, among whom, of course, Dr. Clifford was prominent. So from January onwards till the end of the year I was liable to receive imperative calls to confer, first of all, about the tentative proposals of the Cabinet, and, subsequently, at every turning-point of the painful and precarious progress of the Bill in Parliament. These informal and confidential soundings of Free Church opinion were, from time to time, varied by formal interviews, chiefly with Mr. Birrell, but sometimes with the Prime Minister. So far as the House of Commons was concerned, the crucial difficulty lay with the treatment of the Roman Catholic Schools in view of the necessity of, at least, disarming the opposition, and, if possible, securing the support of the Irish Parliamentary Party. In order to accomplish this feat, the at that time famous Clause 4 of the Bill was devised, which, under cover of complete popular control, sought to give, by indirect means, some sort of guarantee to the Roman Catholics that the denominational character of the teaching staff and the special atmosphere of their schools would be, for the most part, preserved. Another difficulty that was immediately encountered by the Government was the unwillingness of the ordinary Englishman to proceed to extremes. I remember Mr. Birrell telling me soon after the introduction of the Bill that an official at a country railway station had said to him, ' I voted Liberal at the Election, but now I think you are going too far.' And beyond all these difficulties stood the House of Lords! So the proverbial difficulty of navigating between Scylla and Charybdis was, in this case, doubled, in face of the extreme demands of a powerful section of Nonconformists, the determined opposition of Roman Catholics, whose Parliamentary support, or at all events, neutrality, in Parliament was essential, the popular tendency to compromise, and the attitude of the House of Lords under the tutelage of Mr. Balfour.

The Education Controversy.

In these circumstances it was no easy task to pilot the ship of the National Free Church Council. The task became the more difficult when the late Mr. J. Hirst Hollowell formed a special fighting organization to resist all concessions, and, in particular, to defeat the obnoxious Clause 4. Mr. Hollowell had been a Congregational minister at Nottingham and a member of its School Board. He had subsequently given up his ministry to form the Northern Education League, and his ideals for English Education were entirely based upon the model of the United States. It is literally true that Clause 4 killed him, for its defeat was a matter of life and death to him. I remember meeting him in the street during that spring, looking haggard and distraught. I inquired, ' What is the matter? ' ' I am not sleeping,' was his reply. ' Clause 4? ' I asked. ' Yes,' he answered. Shortly after that he had a stroke, and, this being followed by another, he died before the conflict was over. Dr. Clifford was another source of difficulty; for while his usual answer, when sounded as to some concession, was, ' If it be put upon us, we must submit to it, for we cannot expect to get everything at once,' this attitude, in private, did not prevent him from taking immediate and vigorous public action to prevent it from being ' put upon us.' So the swaying battle went on throughout the spring and summer and autumn, the Government being forced into concession after concession, first in the Commons and then in the Lords, in order to convert the elusive Clause 4 into something that could be accepted as a practical guarantee by the Roman Catholics. The process continuously undermined the support of the political Nonconformists, while it did not allay the opposition of the Conservative Party, then entrenched in the House of Lords. So the situation was almost hopeless when the Bill went to the Upper House in the late autumn. The Archbishop of Canterbury took full advantage of the situation with astute statesmanship, directed, in part, to making the Bill tolerable to denominationalists, and, in part, to securing for the National Schools conditions at least as advantageous as those to be tacitly accorded to the Roman Catholics. Thus Lord Crewe, the Liberal Leader in the House of Lords, was placed in an impossible position. A conflict between the two Houses over the mutilated

Bill took place, and on the eve of Christmas 1906 the Government withdrew the measure. I retired to Sidmouth to rest and revise my theological book, now nearing completion. To my surprise I found the Archbishop also there. During the concluding stages of the struggle, he and I had been brought into somewhat close consultation, and now we went over the subject again, walking on the sea-shore. Thereby, notwithstanding our immediate differences, the foundations of a friendship were laid, which has grown ever closer with succeeding years. Perhaps I may sum up my personal impressions of the chief Parliamentary actors with whom I was brought into intimate contact by saying that Sir Henry Campbell-Bannerman was the most robust, consistent, and courageous of them all; Mr. Lloyd George the most adroit; the Archbishop of Canterbury tried with conscientious anxiety to fulfil his trust, not only in the interests of the denominational schools, but, above all, for Religious Education generally; while Mr. Birrell, looking on both sides with somewhat cynical benevolence, seemed to be murmuring, ' A plague on both your Houses! ' amid the harassing perplexities of the conflict.

Some time after the war, I travelled to Cambridge in the same carriage with Mr. Birrell, and we compared notes on the way in which the old controversy had faded away in presence of the stupendous events that had succeeded it. One incident I cannot refrain from recording. I had promised the Annual Assembly of the National Free Church Council that its Executive should be called together directly the Bill was introduced. So, having listened to Mr. Birrell's opening speech on the Monday afternoon, I caused telegrams to be sent out convening the meeting for the Wednesday morning. We met at the Memorial Hall, and I invited Mr. Lloyd George, who was then a member of the Executive, to sit by my side. A lengthy Resolution was moved by Dr. Clifford, expressing gratification with the governing principles and many of the details of the Bill, but objecting to certain elements of compromise in it, and especially to Clause 4. This having been seconded, a hostile amendment was brought forward by the extremer section of the Committee. After the discussion had proceeded for a time, Mr. Hirst Hollowell spoke, and outdid all the others in his denunciation. While intensest in his opposition to Clause 4, he riddled the whole Bill for giving too favourable terms to the Non-provided Schools. To him the Bill appeared to be a mass of ' wounds and bruises and putrifying sores.' But having exhausted his eloquence in denouncing what was *in* the Bill, he went on to pour scorn upon it for what it left out—' A so-called Education Bill that does not deal with the scandalous injustice of the Denominational Training Colleges, maintained by the State and yet allowed to impose denominational tests! ' It should be remarked that the Bill was already portentously long, and that it would have been absolutely impossible to add such a thorny subject to a measure that bristled with controversies. Directly Mr. Hollowell sat down Mr. Lloyd George rose, and after making the best defence he could for all that was in the Bill, he proceeded to say, ' When Mr. Hirst Hollowell calls attention to the flagrant injustice of the Denominational Training Colleges, I am whole-heartedly with him. If he can get the Government to include them in its Bill, I say more strength to his elbow! ' The result was that the Committee spent the rest of its time in hunting for omissions, rather than for criticizing its contents, and eventually Dr. Clifford's Resolution was passed, with only eight dissentients. As Mr. Lloyd George sat down I whispered to him, ' What a strategist you are! ' ' Yes,' he replied, ' and so are you, or you would not have seen it.'

' Contracting Out.'

In 1908 Mr. McKenna, who had succeeded Mr. Birrell at the Board of Education, sought to get round the Roman Catholic difficulty by ' contracting out.' Apart from other drawbacks, the Educational objections to this treatment were serious, for it left the ' contracted-out ' schools apart from the whole structure of National Education, and, as it stood at first, excluded them from participating in Scholarship schemes and from the benefits of all the Municipal provision of medical treatment and social care, which are nowadays rightly held to be indispensable adjuncts of Education. As to this, I ventured to make strong representations to the Minister, and he undertook to remedy this blot upon the Bill. But with the formation of Mr. Asquith's Administration, upon the death of Sir Henry Campbell-Bannerman, Mr. Runciman succeeded to the *damnosa hœreditas* of the controversy, and his first attempt to bring about a settlement had to be abandoned before the year was out. The Education question fell into the background before the conflict over the Licensing Bill, and then over Mr. Lloyd George's Budget.

So the Education question remains unsettled. More than once in recent years I have taken part in private discussions as to a possible solution. I will not discuss the question here, beyond saying that the Educational drawbacks of the Dual System are growingly serious, in view of the recent developments, especially of higher education, aided by scholarships, for Elementary Schools; and that, despite the maintenance of the Non-provided Schools out of public funds, the financial strain upon them is recurrent owing to the ever-increasing demands for the improvement of buildings, the need for amalgamation of schools, and the necessity of an easy passage from these schools to higher grades of Education. Finally, the need of making adequate provision for religious Education, without any violation of the conscience or sacrifice of the interests either of teachers or scholars, is growingly felt by Christians of every denomination, and, I think, by men of good will beyond their borders. It becomes increasingly possible on all these grounds to hope for an eventual settlement by consent, as appreciation of conscientious convictions grows throughout the community. Above all, the golden principle that no child should be allowed to suffer in its education owing to the conscientious convictions of its parents should be borne in mind in all future legislation. Meanwhile the Acts of 1902 and 1903, supplemented by Mr. Fisher's Act of 1917, stand, and, despite all drawbacks, I desire to bear my witness to the way in which all parties have sought to make the best of them, and to the notable advances in all forms of Education that have been made throughout the country under the general schemes of administration that they set up.

Editor of the 'Methodist Times.'

In March 1907 I became the Editor of *The Methodist Times*. During the previous autumn I had been pressed, first of all, by Mr. (afterwards Sir) Henry Holloway and then by Sir Percy Bunting, to accept this post. Their request was supported by Dr. Henry J. Pope, who held strongly that Wesleyan Methodism needed more than one denominational paper, and especially that it was important to maintain an organ which would consistently advocate, with complete freedom, a thoroughly progressive policy in regard to all the concerns of the Church. Somewhat reluctantly I consented to undertake this heavy responsibility as soon as my term of Free Church Presidency was over. So the date was fixed for the middle of March, and being at that time rather severely ill of gastric influenza and the exhaustion that followed upon the exacting labours of the previous year, I was obliged to dictate my first Leader and Editorial Notes to my wife as I lay propped up with pillows in bed. From that day onwards till the end of 1918 I wrote the Leader for every week except two, on one of which owing to restrictions of space and Conference news, there was no Leader, and on one other occasion when, at the request of the Mission House, the Rev. C. W. Andrews contributed a Foreign Missionary article. I also wrote most of the Editorial Notes, though occasionally my contributions were supplemented by my able Sub-Editor, Mr. Arthur Page Grubb. During the sittings of the York Conference in 1908 I found time amid my Presidential duties to write the Leaders and Notes; and when I went to Canada to attend the Oecumenical Conference in 1911, I left articles behind for the seven weeks of my absence. During the whole of my Editorship, I sought, above all, to make the paper the organ of a steadfastly progressive policy, pronouncedly Methodist, yet aiming all the while at closer relations, not only with all the Evangelical Free Churches, but with the Anglican Church as well. The Leaders that stand out most in my memory are the series on the George Jackson case, in which, prior to the Plymouth Conference of 1913, I urged the claims of freedom, without committing myself to the particular conclusions that Mr. Jackson had propounded, and the series on Methodist Union, written in the autumn of 1913, in which I laid down certain conditioning principles, all of which are embodied in the scheme that was dealt with at the Conference of 1927. So far as Anglican relations are concerned, I may be permitted to refer to my attitude on the Enabling Act and its consequences. When the Enabling Bill was produced, I urged in Editorial Notes that Free Churchmen should see in the measure the first step taken by the Anglican Church towards self-government in the spiritual concerns of the Church, and that, therefore, on their own principle, they should support it. On this I received a grateful letter from Viscount Wolmer, who was then acting as a kind of Whip to the Church of England group of M.P.'s, saying that this pronouncement would lead to a complete alteration of their attitude towards Nonconformist legislation. Subsequently I met members of this group on various occasions, and, as the result, they withdrew their opposition to the Leasehold Enfranchisement Bill of the Committee of Privileges and actively promoted its passage through both Houses of Parliament as soon as the end of the war made ordinary legislation once more possible. In December 1918, having carried *The Methodist Times* through the almost fatal period of the war, I handed over my Editorship to younger men, thus becoming free to discharge the heavy duties of Progressive Leader on the London County Council during the years of national reconstruction.

IX.

MY PRESIDENTIAL YEAR

I N 1908 I became President of the Wesleyan Methodist Conference. I had been designated for this office in 1907 by a small majority, for a considerable number of ministers at that time considered me rather a dangerous person, and made energetic efforts to postpone, if not to prevent, my election.

My Presidential Programme.

In entering upon my Presidential duties I had a fairly distinct programme before my mind. In regard to teaching, I set out to enforce the unity of spiritual and social concerns in the wholeness of the Christian life. I sought to do this by emphasizing the significance, and drawing out the implications, of Wesley's insistence upon ' perfect love ' as the ideal of true religion. On the practical side I endeavoured, so far as opportunity was given to me, to come into contact, as Chief Pastor of the Church for the time being, with all the central institutions of Methodism, as, for example, the Theological Colleges and the Schools. While paying special attention to such interests and activities as had hitherto come short of official recognition, though containing the promise of the future, I determined also to concentrate, as far as practicable, my Presidential visits upon the country districts, and with this object arranged with Dr. H. J. Pope a series of conventions throughout the country, and with some of the Chairmen of Synods motor tours throughout their Districts. Finally, I set out to insist somewhat specially upon the responsibility and importance of Methodism as a spiritual factor in the moral and social concerns of national life. Hence I sought to lay down exactly the same spiritual principles at the Southport Holiness Convention, in a three days' conference of the Union for Social Service, which I conducted at Oxford, and at the

Easter gathering of the Wesley Guild in Manchester. In connexion with the last named, it was borne in upon me that I should get the representatives of the Guilds to commit their local branches to clearing off the debt then existing upon the Foreign Missionary Society. They responded enthusiastically to my appeal, and ever since have taken an important share in maintaining the Medical work of the Society.

The conventions throughout the country were largely attended and successful. Their success was increased owing to the help of a band of younger ministers from whom I selected companions on most of my visits. One humorous incident may be recalled. In October, 1908, I held a convention at Norwich, and large numbers came to the services from the whole of East Anglia. One of the railway bills offering cheap fares, held out the following list of attractions for the day—

> Fat Cattle Show,
> Chrysanthemum Show,
> Dog and Kennel Show,
> Hippodrome—twice daily,
> Visit of the Rev. J. Scott Lidgett.

Fighting for the Licensing Bill.

The most dramatic event of the year had to do with the rejection of the Licensing Bill by the House of Lords at the mandate of a caucus of Peers that was held at Lansdowne House. The Government of the day had introduced the Bill in response to powerful pressure, especially of the Christian, and particularly of the Nonconformist, Churches. At the beginning of that year I had myself acted as spokesman of the National Council of Evangelical Free Churches on a deputation to the then Chancellor of the Exchequer, Mr. Asquith, shortly afterwards to become Prime Minister. The main principles of the measure were laid before the Government and formed the basis of their Bill. The Wesleyan Methodist Temperance Committee alone secured more than a million signatures in support of it. The Conference at York, over which I presided, had passed a strong resolution in favour of the Bill, with only a handful of dissentients. So it was the Churches, with the Temperance Societies, that had put this controversial measure upon the Government, had organized support of it throughout the country, and, in particular, the Wesleyan Methodist Church stood officially committed to it through the overwhelming majority of the Conference. So official and overwhelming was this support that as President I arranged and presided over a crowded meeting held in Wesley's Chapel on behalf of the Bill. As the crisis approached, let it be remembered, the claim made was that the Bill should be fairly considered and fully discussed by the House of Lords. Instead of this a party meeting outside the House determined, at the instance of powerful vested interests, to slay the Bill outright and off-hand, without seeking to amend it.

Methodism Will Never Forget or Forgive.

The news of this party political decision, which betrayed moral interests and flaunted the Churches, reached me at the Free Trade Hall just before speaking at the Anniversary of the Manchester Mission. I at once wrote a telegram to the Marquess of Lansdowne, the Conservative Leader in the Lords, to the effect that should the House of Lords reject the Bill on the Second Reading that act ' would never be forgotten or forgiven by the Wesleyan Methodist Church.' I showed the telegram to the Secretary of the Conference, the Rev. John Hornabrook, and, as he confirmed my judgement, I at once dispatched it. Subsequently I read it to the meeting in the Free Trade Hall, and immediately a burst of prolonged applause broke out, the whole audience standing, such as I have never witnessed at any meeting before or since. It will be seen that the demand was not made that the Bill should be passed as it stood, but only that it should be carefully considered, and that the Wesleyan Conference stood so committed to this support that I simply gave expression to its intense conviction on the matter. Yet the small minority of dissentients began to flood *The Methodist Recorder* with protests against the President of the Conference taking part in politics ! This campaign was fostered, for a time, behind the scenes, until, as he himself told me, Dr. Henry J. Pope remonstrated against it, and pointed out its folly by suggesting, 'Don't you see that by doing this you are making him irresistible!' The warning took effect, and on the following Thursday, *The Methodist Recorder* announced that 'This correspondence is now closed.' For some months I was constrained in my platform addresses to expound and enforce the grave responsibility of the Christian Church when supreme moral interests are at issue in the public and political affairs of the nation.

Since considerations of moral judgement and not merely of political expediency are involved, I feel constrained to say that the action of the House of Lords brought nemesis in its track. Flushed by its success in securing the withdrawal of the Education Bill and defeating the Licensing Bill, the House of Lords went on to throw out the Budget. The result was the Parliament Act, and that result was in considerable measure brought about, not for constitutional or political reasons, but because of the indignation of multitudes who would not 'forget or forgive' the contemptuous rejection of a measure that was held by them to be vital to the moral progress of the Nation.

Appreciation of Dr. Pope.

The personal reference just made to Dr. Henry J. Pope makes this a suitable moment to speak of his very remarkable personality, for the form of his intervention in the Licensing Bill controversy was eminently characteristic of his usual methods. He was a great ecclesiastical chess-player, carefully studying all the human pieces with which he had to deal, and the moves that were open to him by skilful use of their idiosyncrasies. I recall that about that time he said to me, 'When I have a scheme in hand I always consider carefully beforehand what I shall do if So-and-so supports me, and what I shall do if So-and-so opposes me.' A man of profound and simple evangelical piety, Dr. Henry J. Pope had all the qualities of a supremely great Civil Servant, exercising practical ascendency, while content to appear as in the background, and using most of the men in the limelight as the instruments of his own far-reaching policies. He used ideas and ideals, not for pulpit and platform oratory, but as the means of getting great measures of evangelistic advance and adaptation carried out. Sometimes, it may be, he was in danger of unduly subordinating ideals to the success of schemes and the successful management of men in their behalf. Yet, when everything is taken account of, his name must certainly be added as the third to those of Dr. Rigg and Hugh Price Hughes, as the three ministers who did most to shape the course of Wesleyan Methodism at the close of the nineteenth and the opening of the twentieth century.

During the first six months of my Presidency, I received much generous kindness from Dr. Rigg, and it was with high appreciation and deep regret that I endeavoured to give an interpretation of his character and life-work, at once just and sympathetic, at his funeral in the early spring of 1909.

More Literary Labours.

It may be of interest to add that returning in the train from the President's Cornish visit, I bought a newspaper at Plymouth which informed me that the University of Aberdeen intended to confer upon me the Honorary Degree of Doctor of Divinity. This generous recognition forestalled the intention of another University, and I was thankful when I learned subsequently that the mover in the matter was the then Professor of Dogmatic Theology, Professor Curtis, and that his action was due to the use he had made in his classes of my book on *The Fatherhood of God.*

During this year and the time immediately following, my thoughts became centred on the Epistle to the Ephesians, and after preaching much upon it, I planned an exposition of it as I travelled to and from the Oecumenical Conference at Toronto. On my return I started lecturing on it at the Settlement, and the volume was published in 1915 under the title *God in Christ Jesus.*

In July 1911 Sir Percy Bunting died somewhat suddenly, and the Editorship of *The Contemporary Review,* which he had carried on with such distinction and success for so many years, became vacant. There was urgent necessity to take immediate steps to meet the situation, for the work of a Monthly Review admits of no cessation. For some time previously Sir Percy Bunting had been accustomed to consult, informally but frequently, Mr. (now Dr.) George P. Gooch and me in regard to many questions concerning the conduct of the *Review*. Hence it became our joint duty to carry on for the time being, with the able and experienced assistance of Miss Evelyn Bunting and of Mr. (now Professor) J. E. G. de Montmorency. We were requested to fulfil this task by Sir John McDougall, then Chairman of the *Contemporary Review Company,* and as this temporary arrangement worked well, it was made permanent after some months, and, in addition to this Joint-editorship, I became Chairman of the Company on the death of Sir John McDougall in the spring of 1917. Throughout all these years it has been our united aim to carry on the *Review* on the lines fixed by Sir Percy Bunting, as an organ of sound and liberal progress,—religious, theological, political, and social—with emphasis on moral and humanitarian concerns, due regard to the interests of Literature, Science, and Art, and with an habitual endeavour to secure the frank discussion of questions of public controversy from different points of view.

During the past few years I have contributed to the *Review* a series of articles on ' Christian Theism in the Light of Modern Thought.' These, with other papers, have been recently published as a separate volume, under the title, *God, Christ, and the Church.*

A Visit to Canada.

In September 1911 I made my only trip across the Atlantic, in order to attend the Oecumenical Methodist Conference in Toronto. Hitherto the pressure of home duties had prevented me from accepting various invitations to the United States. In the company of a party of friends, which included the late Rev. Enoch Salt and the Rev. H. T. Smart, we spent the fortnight previous to the Conference in a tour to the Rockies, visiting places of importance and interest on the journey out and back to Toronto. What impressed me most vividly—apart from the interest of scenery and towns,—was the close inter-relationship between Britain and the Dominion brought about by personal relationships. As examples of this I may mention that, after preaching in the Metropolitan Church immediately after my arrival in Toronto, the first person to greet me as I came down from the pulpit was an elderly man who had been a church member at Old Southwark Chapel, and, later in the same day, one who had known me in my early ministry at Southport. Subsequently, as I was walking by the Bow River near Banff, a lady and gentleman suddenly appeared through an almost blinding blizzard, and greeted me. Said the gentleman, ' The last time I heard you preach was at Weston-super-Mare.' Said the lady, ' And the last time I heard you preach was at Morte Hoe.' In connexion with the Oecumenical Conference, I may perhaps record the fact that I was commissioned to write the Encyclical Letter, which the Conference sent out to be read in the Methodist Churches throughout the world at the beginning of the following year.

X.
WELSH DISESTABLISHMENT AND CHURCH REUNION

EARLY in 1914 I became Joint Honorary Secretary of the National Council of Evangelical Free Churches, and many of my more recent public activities have been directly or indirectly connected with that post. For years I had been responsible for the work of the Education Committee of the Council, and from the time of Dr. F. B. Meyer's appointment as Honorary Secretary of the Council in 1910 I had been regularly, though informally, called upon to advise with him in regard to all the public questions that called for the Council's attention. Moreover, in recent years, I had taken an increasing part in the work of public bodies concerned with moral and humanitarian interests. For example, I had been a very active member of the Congo Reform Association, had co-operated with the Armenian Committee, and with other Societies for the Protection of Subject and Backward Races, and was Chairman for years of the London Temperance Council. Now Dr. Meyer made it a condition of his continuing to be responsible for the work of the National Free Church Council that I should be officially associated with him, in order that I might be formally entrusted with the responsibility of advising in regard to public questions as they arose. I need hardly say how highly I regarded the privilege of this co-operation with Dr. Meyer, a privilege which I enjoyed until his retirement from office in 1920, when I became sole Honorary Secretary of the Council in association with the newly-appointed and energetic General Secretary, the Rev. Thomas Nightingale. This office I continue to hold.

Welsh Disestablishment.

About this time the Welsh Disestablishment Bill was

introduced into the House of Commons by the then Home Secretary, Mr. McKenna. While convinced of the justice of the Bill from the political standpoint, and of its beneficence in the spiritual interest of the Episcopal Church in Wales, I was greatly concerned by the severity of the original proposals of the Bill in respect of Disendowment. I felt deeply that the true policy to be pursued, from the Christian standpoint, should aim, not at crippling, but at increasing the efficiency of the Welsh Church. While Endowments that were demonstrably connected with State Establishment must be taken away, existing interests should be, not merely equitably, but generously considered. Breathing space, in regard to finances, should be provided for the reconstitution of the Church, and wherever serious doubt existed as to the nature of the Endowments, the Church should have the benefit of that doubt. Being deeply concerned about this, I felt constrained to take some personal action in the matter, not only in the columns of *The Methodist Times,* but with Members of Parliament, taking care to act throughout in a strictly personal capacity.

With this object in view I went down to the House of Commons one afternoon, and as I entered the Lobby met Sir Henry Lunn. I found that he was engaged in the same endeavour, so I at once joined forces with him in the constitution and work of a special committee on the subject, which he called into being. The late Lord Justice Fry accepted the Chairmanship of this Committee, Sir Henry Lunn acted as Honorary Secretary, and among its members were Bishop Gore (then Bishop of Oxford) and Canon Hensley Henson (now Bishop of Durham) of the Church of England, Dr. Campbell Morgan and Dr. James Hope Moulton of the Free Churches. At the outset of the discussions considerable differences of opinion existed. The Chairman acted with strictly judicial impartiality throughout; but while some desired only minor alterations, if any, in the Bill, others, including some prominent Nonconformists, were opposed to any disendowment whatever. Gradually, however, the view that Bishop Gore and I put forward prevailed—namely, that the

Tithes must go, and that they should be appropriated to the Educational and Social objects set forth in the Bill, but that the bulk of the other Endowments should remain the property of the disestablished Church.

An Embarrassing Situation.

Eventually a Report, in this general sense, was adopted, Bishop Gore and I being appointed to speak for the Committee at a Deputation to wait upon the Prime Minister, Mr. Asquith. Mr. Asquith at once appointed a date for the reception of the Committee. On the eve of addressing him, however, I found myself placed in a great difficulty. I received an invitation to attend a Breakfast on the morning of the day that had been fixed for the deputation. Imagining that the meeting was called to consider measures of conciliation, I accepted the invitation. To my surprise and embarrassment I found myself, on arriving, in the midst of a large gathering consisting of several Members of the Government, Liberal Members of Parliament, journalists, and others, convened to give impetus to a popular movement in support of the Bill, the whole Bill, and nothing but the Bill. After certain addresses in explanation of the position had been given, the Chairman of the Liberation Society (the late Dr. Massie) made a speech denouncing ' Weak-kneed Nonconformists,' and Dr. Clifford followed, deploring their weakness. Unexpectedly I was called upon to follow them, and was, therefore, put upon my mettle to outline, in common honesty, the views I was to lay before Mr. Asquith that very afternoon. So I opened my speech to the following effect, ' As I look round this gathering I find that none of those with whom I am at present acting is present. I must, therefore, conclude that in this meeting I am the only " weak-kneed Nonconformist," whom Dr. Massie has denounced and Dr. Clifford has deplored. However this may be, I will certainly not be weak-kneed on the present occasion.' I then proceeded to support the view previously expressed, that considering the nature of the Tithes and of the extended uses to which the original Endowments had been applied by the ancient Church, the charge of sacrilege in applying them to humane objects could not be sustained. But I argued on the lines of Mr. Gladstone's policy in regard to Irish disendowment, that the Welsh Bill, as it stood, was harsh and ungenerous, and that it should be amended in important particulars, some of which I specified. I was heard in silence, though there was indignation in certain quarters. In the afternoon, Bishop Gore and I advanced substantially the same views to the Prime Minister, and our contentions were received, not only with the utmost courtesy, but with the promise, sympathetically given, of careful consideration by the Government. Eventually, as is well known, the controversy was ended by Mr. Lloyd George after the war, on terms even more generous than we had proposed. The result has been, as is now confessed by the whole body of its members from the Archbishop of Wales downwards, that the Welsh Episcopal Church has not only had a fair start, but that it has entered upon an era of greatly increased prosperity by the removal of a legitimate grievance outside and by the enjoyment of full self-government within its borders.

Work in War-time.

The outbreak of the Great War laid great responsibilities upon me, as Joint Honorary Secretary of the National Free Church Council, in August 1914. Dr. Meyer was in America, and many other leading men were scattered upon holidays. For some days previous to Sir Edward (now Viscount) Grey's great speech in the House of Commons on that fateful August Bank Holiday, strenuous efforts had been made, from certain quarters, to hold Britain back from any policy that would involve an alliance with Russia. In particular, Dr. Robertson Nicoll had been persuaded to write a strong article in this strain in the previous week's *British Weekly*. The position was serious. So, by arrangement, I spent that Monday afternoon in the Inner Lobby of the House of Commons, and was supplied, at intervals, by the late Sir Joseph Compton-Rickett with instalments of Sir Edward Grey's speech as it proceeded. Directly it was finished, I took a hansom-cab and drove to Dr. Nicoll's residence in

Hampstead, where I explained to him the position, as it had been unfolded by the Foreign Secretary, with the result that he prepared himself, at once, to support the National policy in that week's *British Weekly*. A little later on, I spent the greater part of two days at Lambeth Palace, as a member of the Committee that prepared the Reply to the German Theologians in regard to the war. While the Committee was greatly indebted to the Dean of Wells (Dr. J. Armitage Robinson) and Dr. J. H. Shakespeare for their work in drafting, the most conspicuous service of all was rendered by the Archbishop of Canterbury himself, not only by his chairmanship in general, but by the remarkable felicity with which he gave the final expression to some of the most critical paragraphs of the document. In justice, however, to all concerned, and in view of the ill-founded charges that have often been brought against the Churches, it should be added that up to the last moment they had striven for peace. They had organized the exchange of visits between British and German representatives of the Churches to promote better relations between the two respective nations. Only a few days before the Declaration of War, I had drafted a letter on behalf of the National Free Church Council, to accompany the message of the Archbishop of Canterbury for communication to the Christian Peace Conference that was actually assembled at Constance when war broke out.

It is beyond the scope of these Reminiscences to discuss the causes which made the actions of the Churches ineffectual, or their attitude during the war. It must suffice to say that many of us gave unstinted service to the cause of peace during the anxious years that preceded the war, and that whole-hearted support has been given to the League of Nations by the Churches, not only since its foundation, but from the first moment that its formation was proposed. One other personal reminiscence of the war should be added. With the outbreak of hostilities it became necessary to provide for religious ministrations to the wounded who began to arrive at hospitals throughout the country. I at once wrote a letter to every Free Church Council in the country, requesting the Secretary to convene without delay a meeting of all the Free Church ministers within his area. Each of these meetings should arrange a panel of voluntary chaplains for service to the wounded, forwarding their names to me. These I submitted day by day to the War Office, with the result that by the end of the first month of the war, nearly 500 Free Church Chaplains had been approved by the War Office, and the immediate necessities of the situation had been met.

Federal Council of Free Churches.

At this point it is necessary to anticipate future events and to speak of the formation of the Federal Council of the Evangelical Free Churches. In 1916 Dr. J. H. Shakespeare became President of the National Free Church Council. Three years previously he had outlined a proposal for the establishment of a ' Free Church of England.' At that time his view was that the historic differences of the Evangelical Free Churches were by this time out of date, that the needs of the age demanded their fusion, and that, in particular, the age-long antithesis between the Religion of Authority and the Religion of the Spirit demanded such fusion, if the witness of the latter was to be made effectual. At the outset Dr. Shakespeare sought my support for his proposal, and, up to a point, I assisted him. But I pointed out that any Christian movement towards unity and reunion was intrinsically universal, and that just in proportion as his endeavour become successful, it would rely upon and give impetus to ideals and influences that would throw down his proposed limitation and seek the complete reunion of the Christian Church. In the end Dr. Shakespeare came himself to adopt this point of view, and in the closing years of his activity —shortened, alas! by painful and incapacitating illness—he devoted all his great powers to the realization of this larger ideal.

In 1916, however, he still adhered to the more limited plan, and devoted his Inaugural Address, as President of the National Free Church Council, to propounding and advocating this scheme. A strong Committee was appointed to consider it.

Deputations were appointed to wait upon the Annual Assemblies and Conferences of the Free Churches, and all of them agreed to take part in the inquiry. A preliminary conference was held at Mansfield College, Oxford, in the autumn of 1916; and this was followed by an adjourned meeting held at The Leys School, Cambridge, in the spring of 1917. Two principal Committees were appointed, one to draw up a Declaration of Faith, the other to prepare a Constitution. Dr. Carnegie Simpson acted as Chairman of the former, and I presided over the latter. As the result the Federal Council was established on its present basis, the Declaration and the Scheme being adopted with practical unanimity by all the constituent denominations.

This is not the place to speak of the relations between the Federal Council and the National Free Church Council, save to say, that, while their fusion has so far proved impracticable, and may be undesirable, they have acted from the first in close association and with mutual helpfulness. Thus it came about that when the larger proposal of the Lambeth Conference was made, a representative body was in existence that could focus the mind of all the Free Churches upon the subject, and could undertake without prejudice to the rights and responsibilities of the denominations, a preliminary investigation of the issues that were raised.

Movement Towards Reunion.

The movement towards the larger Reunion had been inaugurated early in 1914, when an influential deputation from the Churches of the United States visited this country to propose a World Conference on Faith and Order. This deputation, of course, made an immediate approach to the Archbishop of Canterbury, and met an influential gathering of Free Churchmen at a dinner, which Dr. Meyer and I arranged. After this visit certain preliminary Committees of investigation were appointed, and as the result a joint *Interim Committee on Faith and Order* was set up, which got to work just as the war broke out, and held many prolonged sittings till the end of 1917.

On the Anglican side, the then Bishop of Winchester (Dr. Talbot), the then Bishop of Oxford (Dr. Gore), and Professor H. L. Goudge were perhaps the most active members; on the Free Church side, Dr. Shakespeare, Dr. Garvie, and I. The late Bishop of Bath and Wells (Dr. Kennion) acted as Chairman throughout, and brought to the discussions the advantages of his deep spirituality and his wide experience, not only in England, but in Australia. It proved easy to draw up a unanimous Statement in regard to the Faith. But the discussions of Order were prolonged and difficult. In the end a Report was agreed upon which did a good deal to prepare the way of the Lambeth Appeal, and indicated the issues that have since arisen out of it.

Meanwhile, a number of the most eminent of the Evangelical Clergy had not been inactive. Quite apart from any question of the proposed World Conference the various considerations that became most influential during the war prompted them to bring about Conferences held successively in London and in Oxford, which led to the publication of a volume of Essays in 1919 entitled, *Towards Reunion* (Macmillan & Co.). To that volume I contributed the opening Paper, ' Reunion and the Advancement of Christ's Kingdom.' I have included this article in a volume of collected essays, theological and ecclesiastical, which Messrs. Hodder & Stoughton published last autumn under the title, *God, Christ, and the Churches*. About the same time I made a suggestion in *The Contemporary Review* that National and Diocesan Councils should be created, on which Anglicans and Free Churchmen should serve, for religious as well as for social purposes. This suggestion was adopted in the Lambeth Appeal, and has been carried out here and there, notably in Manchester. Probably a more general endeavour would have been made to carry it into effect had not the C.O.P.E.C. Conference sought to bring a somewhat similar, though more limited, organization into existence.

Results of the Lambeth Appeal.

The issue of all these and other similar movements is too well-known to need enlarged mention here. *The Appeal to all Christian People,* issued by the Lambeth Conference in August 1920, opened a new era in the relations between the Episcopal and the non-Episcopal Churches throughout the world. Whatever may be the merits and prospects of the precise plan of the Appeal, the spirit which animated it, as well as the loftiness and breadth of its outlook will prove epoch-making, whatever delays and set-backs it may encounter. Throughout the succeeding years I served, not only upon the Joint Committee that was constituted for the preliminary consideration of the Appeal, but upon its Sub-Committee. During the two concluding years, 1923-1925, it fell to me, as successor to Dr. J. D. Jones in the Moderatorship of the Federal Council, to act as Foreman of the Free Church Members of the Sub-Committee. The series of Reports that were prepared and presented represent an achievement, which must needs be the starting-point of any subsequent endeavours to promote Reunion. For the purpose of these Reminiscences, however, it must suffice to say that the memory of the spiritual influences that attended our prolonged discussions will always be treasured by every one who took part in them. Relations of complete mutual confidence and intimacy were established that will prove lasting, appreciation, as well as knowledge, of contested points of view was brought about, and while grave issues remain for the present undetermined and possibly insoluble, the positive agreements that were reached must go far to give strength and precision to a unity of heart and mind, which must eventually find expression in the life and organization of the whole Church of Christ. Would that such spiritual conditions could become widespread throughout the world! As I write, there is increased hope that this may be the case, for the Conference that was proposed in 1914 has just been held at Lausanne, and, while the same differences and difficulties emerged there, that have been encountered previously, the Conference decided upon an intensive and extensive campaign for their friendly discussion throughout the world.

During this period I completed, in my scanty leisure, an exposition of the Epistle to the Hebrews, which was published in the autumn of 1921 under the title *Sonship and Salvation*. In this volume I endeavoured to show that even in an Epistle which deals with the dominant theme of priesthood and sacrifice, the exposition and explanation are governed throughout by the conception of the Fatherly-filial relationship as the distinctive feature of the Christian Faith.

XI.
LONDON COUNTY COUNCIL PROBLEMS

Leader of the L.C.C. Progressives.

IN March, 1918, I was elected, with surprising unanimity, to the Leadership of the Progressive Party on the London County Council, in succession to Sir John Benn, who resigned on the ground of serious ill-health. I had been Leader of the Party on the Education Committee since 1913. A war-time Coalition between the Municipal Reformers and the Progressives had been brought about at the beginning of 1917. This arrangement had been very actively supported by Sir John Benn, and generally approved by Mr. Harry Gosling, then Leader of the Labour Party on the Council, though he himself cautiously abstained from joining it. When the project was first mooted to me I pointed out that joint responsibility for policy on the Council would involve joint responsibility for it to the electors. The Coalition, however, had the immediate advantages of agreement in upholding the essential services during the final strain of the war, while fulfilling patriotic demands, of securing practically unanimous agreement, for the time being, with Mr. Fisher's Education policy and of making friendly co-operation possible in determining a united programme of reconstruction possible after the war.

A Progressive Reconstruction Policy.

In October, 1918, I took the lead by publishing a progressive policy of reconstruction in *The Contemporary Review*. The programme I outlined contained as its principal items, the reform of London Government, Housing and Slum clearance, together with advance in all grades of Education and all types of Schools. All these main objects were subsequently adopted by the Municipal Reform Party and set forward in their Manifesto for the Election of March 1919. Union in the essentials of a Reconstruction Policy led, as its inevitable corollary, to mutual forbearance at the election. In the absence of serious questions in dispute and of the apathy that succeeded the war, the election aroused comparatively little interest. Only a small proportion of the Electors went to the poll, and I was returned for the third time as member for Rotherhithe by a majority of nearly two to one over my half-hearted Labour Party opponents. The new Council secured the appointment of a Royal Commission on London Government, set on foot a great Housing Scheme, in partnership with the Government, on the lines laid down by Mr. Addison, the Minister of Health, and established a complete system of Day Continuation Schools, as the first and last, so it turned out, attempt to carry out that provision of Mr. Fisher's Education Act. A far-reaching scheme of general Educational Advance was also laid out, which has formed the basis of the Council's policy ever since. Some explanation of all these projected reforms is necessary.

The Need for Reform.

The need for the Reform of London Government was created by the fact that whereas in 1889 the bulk of the people of London resided within the County, the immense growth of Greater London has led to a shrinkage of population within the County and such vast overflows into the Counties of Middlesex, Surrey, and Essex, that in 1925 the population of the County was 4,500,000, while the population of Greater London outside the County amounted to 3,000,000. Great multitudes work within the County and sleep outside it. Hence the essential services of Transport, Drainage, Electrical Supply, Housing, Public Health, and Education outreach the County and ought to be dealt with by a Municipal Authority, whose area should not be less than that of the Metropolitan Police District of Greater London. The only alternative is the multiplication of *ad hoc* authorities, with the result that Municipal responsibility and power will be reduced to a minimum. The case was laid before a Royal Commission, but was rejected owing largely to the opposition of the County of Middlesex. As a result of this defeat composite and undemocratic Boards have been established to deal with Traffic and Electricity. Housing Estates have been planted beyond the County—as at Becontree —under the management of the L.C.C., which impose administrative burdens for Education, Public Health, &c., on local authorities that are reluctant and scarcely able to bear them, while it remains impossible to devise the comprehensive system of Education that London sorely needs.

Housing Schemes.

The Housing Policy of the Council has been carried out successively under the Addison, Chamberlain, and Wheatley Schemes for financial partnership between the State and the local authority.

I do not think the public realizes how vast the Housing undertaking of the L.C.C. has been. Up to September 30, 1927, the total capital expenditure since the War had been £22,628,941, while the future capital expenditure to which the Council is committed amounts to £16,750,000. When I add that the total capital expenditure from the beginning to March 1919 was only £5,815,523 it will be seen that the Council has done its utmost to deal with the pressing need of additional houses. Already 21,030 houses have been completed, an additional 13,272 are in hand, and another 14,724 are projected, making a total of 49,026.

By far the largest of the new housing estates is at Becontree, in Essex, which, when the programme is completed, will provide for a population of more than 100,000 people.

Smaller, though important schemes have been carried out at Bellingham and Downham, near Catford, and at Roehampton, near Putney, while new schemes are being set on foot in the neighbourhood of Edgware, in Hertfordshire, and at Morden in the South West of London. The completion of this programme would have been more rapid and would have been carried out at a smaller cost had it not been for the shortage of available labour.

Building Trades Unions' Policy.

The Building Trades Unions resisted all pressure from the Government to allow intensive training to be given to Ex-Service men after the war. They were afraid that some change of policy in regard to Housing might prevent the completion of the National programme and throw this diluted labour upon the Unions for support. No arguments or persuasion could shake this lack of confidence. The consequence has been that at various times the L.C.C. has been held up for lack of bricklayers, plasterers and other workmen.

Some of these estates, notably Becontree, are outside the County of London and, as has been said, the responsibility for the local government of these areas does not rest upon the L.C.C., but in the case of Becontree on Essex, and of Edgware on Hertfordshire.

The shortage of houses has greatly hampered the Council in dealing with insanitary areas, yet twenty-two of these are at present in hand, covering ninety-one acres and dealing with a population of nearly 26,000.

Some Drawbacks on New Estates.

That there are certain drawbacks about these new estates cannot be denied. They tend to gather together a population exclusively of one social class. The fact that so few sites are available within the County of London has meant that the inhabitants of these new estates have in most cases to travel a long way to and from their work. Hence the cost of living is increased.

Moreover, although the community bears a considerable proportion of the loss, since economic rents cannot be imposed, the cost of living in these new estates and of travel to and from work prevent the houses from being occupied by the very poor, while in view of the increase in the population the exodus has not been sufficient to effect any substantial improvement in the overcrowding of the congested districts.

The necessity of devoting all the available capital to actual outlay on houses has made it impossible to supply the new

estates with public institutions other than Elementary Schools.
There has been, however, one important exception. Soon after
the Housing Policy was undertaken I introduced a deputation of
Clergy and Ministers to the Housing Committee, and as a
result of their representations the L.C.C. obtained permission
from the Ministry of Health to reduce the cost of sites for places
of worship. This valuable concession has been taken advantage
of by the Wesleyan Methodist Church at Becontree and at
Downham. An arrangement has been entered into between all
the Free Churches not to compete with one another on these new
estates—a very valuable instalment of the efforts to avoid
overlapping, to which all these denominations are committed.

Yet this great progress, with the additions made to it by the
City Corporation, by the Borough Councils, and by private
enterprise has hardly sufficed to make good the shortage caused
by the war and the increase of population. It has done
comparatively little to remedy overcrowding in the congested
neighbourhoods, or to make it possible to deal on an adequate
scale with insanitary areas. Yet the London County Council has
steadily gone forward with a policy, the magnitude of which is
unexampled and which has made use to the full of the supplies
of labour that have been available.

The development of Education by the Council since the war
has been so comprehensive and continuous that Mr. Trevelyan,
when Labour Minister of Education, declared publicly that his
task would have been easy were all the Education Authorities
throughout the country like the London County Council.

An Educational Reverse.

One great Educational reverse has taken place—the downfall
of the Day Continuation Schools. These schools were
handicapped at the start. Many of the great employers welcomed
them, in some cases housing them and in others cheerfully
co-operating with them in their business arrangements. But
they undoubtedly caused difficulties to small employers, which
could only have been accepted and surmounted had public
opinion been strongly behind them. Then they had to be carried

on in hired and often unsatisfactory buildings, which compared badly with the spacious Day Schools to which the pupils had been accustomed. Moreover, the curriculum had been somewhat hastily devised, and was intended to make as great a change as possible from ordinary Elementary Education. Hence there was a certain lack of practical utility, and imperfect classification of the pupils. The Teaching Staff, having been suddenly recruited, was only partially satisfactory. As the result of all these drawbacks discipline was sometimes defective. Worst of all, the period of commercial depression and consequent unemployment supervened, and many parents believed that the chances of their children finding employment were damaged by the obligation to attend these schools.

This grievance was intensified by the fact that, owing to the lack of unification, the new law was not acted upon by the Local Education Authorities of Greater London, with the result that parents in the County complained that their children were being supplanted by out-county children, who could be employed for whole, instead of part-time. Finally, Parliament had tied up the curriculum by insisting that a large proportion of the time-table should be taken up by physical exercises. Hence working-class mothers complained that ' they wouldn't mind if their children were learning anything useful, but they did object to their time being spent in learning dancing.'

Attempts to remedy these drawbacks were under consideration, when the Election of March, 1922, took place. I myself put forward proposals, which would have removed them, by seeking powers to make the curriculum more practical, and to give the pupils the choice of compulsory attendance in the evening, when the daytime was proved to be inconvenient.

Labour Opposition.

But on the eve of the Election the Municipal Reform Party pledged themselves, to the dismay of their educationists, that, if returned to power, they would close the Schools. The Labour Party promised that if the Schools were continued they would provide maintenance grants for the children. So the

Progressive Candidates were left to bear the brunt of the storm, which fell upon me with the utmost force, as their Leader, and because I had supported Sir Robert Blair, the Education Officer of the County Council, in a speech, when he explained the Scheme to a stormy meeting in the Bermondsey Town Hall.

Meanwhile the local Labour Party had organized a tremendous attack upon me—partly clever and partly unscrupulous. In particular, they brigaded the unemployed and misrepresented me as being their enemy, although I had been the proposer of the appointment by the L.C.C. of an Unemployment Committee to co-operate with the Borough Councils in finding work of various kinds by making up the arrears caused by the war. All these and other attacks being held to be insufficient to dislodge me, a final stroke was devised which proved effective. A local Labour dispute on the Waterside—called by the Employers a strike and by the Employees a lock-out—had put some hundreds of men temporarily out of work. The foreman of the works was a Wesleyan. I did not know of its existence, and spent the day before the Election peacefully at Lambeth Palace discussing Reunion. A meeting of the unemployed was hastily called at the Rotherhithe Town Hall, and it was given out that because the foreman of the firm was a Wesleyan, I was ' blacklegging ' for the employers. This charge was spread along the Waterside that evening, with the result that on the day of the Election my workers returned to the Committee Rooms to announce that the situation was hopeless, and I was heavily defeated. Subsequently, the then Conservative Member for Rotherhithe publicly took credit for having induced a number of Conservative voters to support the Labour candidates as a protest against the refusal of the Central Municipal Reform Committee to oppose my re-election.

Immediately upon my defeat in Rotherhithe I was offered and accepted an Aldermanship of the London County Council. On election to this office I was welcomed with gratifying cordiality by the Council as a whole. During the last six years I have continued to take an active part in the general work of the Council. The work of reconstruction after the war has been carried on with vigour and public spirit, though under the restrictions imposed, as I have previously explained, by the present condition of London Government. These years have not been marked by any acute controversy upon the Council, and, therefore, no grave issues have been submitted to the judgement of the electors.

Defeat of the Progressives.

In 1925 the Progressive Party shared the depressed failure of the Liberal Party, and sank to be the third party on the Council. The very success of the Progressives in communicating their ideals to the Municipal Reformers on the right and to the Labour Party on the left has told to their disadvantage as a Party. This triumph in the realm of ideals has been accompanied by a growing tendency, accentuated by the rise and intransigence of the Labour Party, to extend the divisions and organization of the national political parties to include the municipal affairs of London. Such intrusion of extraneous party interests into the realm of local administration is, in many respects, greatly to be regretted, and as my term of municipal service draws to an end, I am glad to have been associated for thirty years with continuous endeavours to promote great issues upon their intrinsic merits, and to be relieved of association with any attempt to subordinate these issues to the extraneous interests of party organization and propaganda.

Success Against Greyhound Racing.

The work of the Council during the last three years has been carried forward with great activity and on a high level of efficiency. For that very reason it has been peaceful and unexciting. It was my privilege last December to lead the Council in opposing the establishment of a greyhound racing track at the Crystal Palace. This opposition, taken in conjunction with that of the City Corporation, led by Sir Ernest Lamb, and of the Boroughs in the neighbourhood of the Palace, has been successful not only in regard to the Palace, but also in arousing a national and Parliamentary movement to put down this most demoralizing evil.

L.C.C. Labour Members and the Strike.

A great test was applied to the Council by the General Strike of May 1926. An Emergency Committee was formed to carry on the essential services during the crisis, and I took a very active part in the work of this Committee. The Labour Party declined co-operation and held aloof, deeming their allegiance to the Trades Union Council to be an obligation that took precedence over their responsibilities to the citizens of London. Mr. Snowden recently appealed for a Labour Party victory on the ground that the capture of the London County Council would be a big step towards bringing about ' Socialism in our time.' It is to be hoped that the electors of London will steadily refuse power to a party which cannot be trusted, in a crisis, to set the safety and civilization of London above the behests of outside organizations pursuing sectional aims and adopting, on occasion, revolutionary methods to advance them.

Elected to the London University Senate.

In the autumn of 1922 I was elected by Convocation to the Senate of the University of London, to fill a vacancy caused by the death of Sir Albert Rollit. The work of the Senate during the past five years has been of exceptional importance owing in part to the remarkable expansion and the increase of students since the war, but still more to the pending reconstruction of the Senate under the Act of Parliament recently passed, and also to the scheme, now in hand, for establishing an adequate headquarters for the administration of the University upon the Bloomsbury site. In all these matters I have taken an active concern.

The University of London has grown to be the largest in the world, and has features that distinguish it from any other university. In addition to its internal side, which includes the Incorporated Colleges and the London Medical Schools, its external side connects it with educational institutions and with students throughout the British Empire. The difficulty of combining the internal and external sides has been successfully overcome. The scheme for developing the new site as an adequate and imposing centre for the administration of the University and for the accommodation of certain of its schools and institutions is being shaped at the present time. When this has been carried out London will be provided with a suitable outward and visible sign of the existence of its University, though even then the number of its scattered colleges and its world-wide activities will prevent its greatness from being visualized, as is the case with Oxford and Cambridge, and with the local universities in this country and elsewhere. Throughout the future the University of London will have a distinctive genius of its own, and will serve, in particular, as a foremost influence in cementing the unity of the British Empire by means of the common ideals and facilities of higher education.

Member of the Athenaeum Club.

In 1923 the famous Athenæum Club prepared to celebrate its centenary, by giving power to its Committee to nominate fifty new members in commemoration of the event. Owing to the kind thought of my valued friend, Sir Thomas Barlow, my name was brought forward, and on the nomination of the Archbishop of Canterbury, seconded by the Archdeacon of Westminster, Dr. R. H. Charles, I was included in the list of these privileged people.

At a somewhat earlier date I had been appointed Chairman of the Executive Committee of the Central Council for District Nursing in London, my old colleague and friend, Sir William Collins, K.C.V.O., M.D., being the Chairman of the Council. In this office, I have taken my part in co-ordinating the work of the various nursing associations, and in securing that an adequate supply of fully trained district nurses is available for the poor throughout Greater London.

XII.
CLOSING OBSERVATIONS

I T is time to bring these Reminiscences to a conclusion. In doing so, perhaps I may be allowed to make a few general observations without laying myself open to any charge of egotism. Some people have charged me in past years with ' having too many irons in the fire.' Others have asked how I have managed to get through so much work, and to discharge such multifarious duties. They have suggested that I must needs ' burn the midnight oil.' Many have probably condemned me for giving so much time and strength to what they regard as merely secular affairs. Before coming to the most important questions, I may answer that my work has been made possible by great regularity of habits, by the power of quickly switching off attention from one subject to another, and not least of all, by the acquired habit of very swift preparation of sermons, speeches, and articles, with a large trust in the spontaneity of the moment. This last has certain incidental risks and drawbacks, due for the most part to conditions of health, mood, and freshness at the moment when the call to speak arises. There is rest and refreshment in change of occupation. Often I have replied to questions, ' The L.C.C. is my golf.'

Providential Calling.

Coming, however, to the main point, I would say that my life has *grown* through a combination of inward urge and outward opportunity, which I have regarded as indications of a providential calling. Hence the internal unity of a sense of calling and of a governing objective have saved me, for the most part, from the jarring competition of claims, and from the distraction of conflicting responsibilities imposed from without. The chief strain upon me has arisen, not from manifold activities, but from the primary concern of having to bear, often alone, wearing financial burdens for sustaining many indispensable agencies in a very poor district out of sight. I have steadily refused all along to adopt methods of advertisement, which I think inflict injury upon the self-respect of the poor, vulgarize the work itself, and may easily damage the spirit of those who are driven by financial pressure to advertise themselves in order to support their work. The internal sense of unity, by which I have been sustained, has been due to my conception of the Wholeness of Life, of the Wholeness of Society, and of the Wholeness of the Church. This threefold Wholeness has for me been the immediate consequence of the Fatherhood of God as revealed by and in our Lord Jesus Christ.

A Threefold Wholeness.

1. The Wholeness of Life. The distinction between the sacred and the secular is false, in so far as it is made a hard-and-fast separation. The true division is between life in and for God, and life, or what is left of it, apart from God. Fellowship with God in life and service, if completed, carries with it sympathy with and support given to the whole of His purposes for men. His purpose embraces the perfecting of human personalities—in body, mind, and spirit—the perfecting of society, and the handling of our earthly environment so that it may be made increasingly the instrument of bringing about this individual and social perfecting. No activity and interest that is bound up with the welfare of men can possibly fall outside the scope of the Kingdom of God. The superiority of the spiritual life is shown, not in the interests it excludes, but in those that it is enabled to include, purify, and harmonize within the supreme relationship to ' the God and Father of our Lord Jesus Christ.'

2. Hence, also, the Wholeness of human Society and the call to rise above sectional aims and success by a spirit of self-giving that transcends the distinctions of class, party, denomination, and in the last resort, of nationality itself.

3. The Wholeness of the Church. This means that the

followers of Christ are bound together in a spiritual unity that cannot be destroyed by ecclesiastical barriers, by sectarian denials of it, by doctrinal differences, or by the consequent failure to give to this unity final and complete expression.

Yet this inward and spiritual unity demands outward and corporate expression, as far as loyalty to truth—as truth is conceived by faith and therefore is to be maintained by faithfulness—will permit. Even conscientious differences of belief should not be held in a sectarian spirit or maintained by ruthless controversy. All maintenance of differences should be carried out, not only for the sake of ultimate unity, but in the spirit that searches for, rejoices in, and seeks to manifest that internal unity of fellowship in Christ, which happily is not destroyed by even the serious errors in respect to doctrine and usage, which the limitations of the human mind for the time being involve. Here we must beware lest our perception of the ' mote,' or perhaps even the ' beam ' in our brother's eye should cause us to overlook the beam in our own eye.

For the time being it would appear inevitable that the Religion of Authority and the Religion of the Spirit should stand out in opposition to one another. Each is vitiated by grave defects. The burden of tradition borne by the former not only includes many unchristian errors, but involves the suppression of the free and vital activities of personal faith. The danger of the latter arises from undue subjectivity and careless independence of what has been brought down to us by tradition, just because it is in some way or other bound up either with apostolic truth or with abiding spiritual needs. Hence the existing tension between Authority and Freedom, while inevitable, may well be providentially ordered, or at all events tolerated, in order that the interaction of the two may serve the wider ends of spiritual life, until the opposition can be transcended in the larger truth, which will correct as well as comprehend them both.

The Policy of Methodist Union.

It is from this standpoint that I regard the policy of Methodist

Reunion. By the providence of God Methodism at its best represents a most remarkable enshrining of Apostolic and Catholic truth in a living Evangelic experience. Its genius enables it to hold these two elements duly balanced, not only as its own privilege, but as a trust for the universal Church. The demands of ecclesiastical organization, while important, are subordinate, and if unduly pressed, would injure just that which is most distinctive and vital in the ' Charisma ' of Methodism. The present controversy in the Anglican Church shows how precarious is the comprehensiveness of an external system, when it holds together grave antagonisms of doctrine, principle, and temper. Methodism, as it contemplates the union of its three branches in this country, is free from any apprehension of serious danger in this direction. It must not subordinate and sacrifice the ' unity of the spirit ' to controversies about authority and organization, when the claims of these are reasonably satisfied. Methodism, if united by the spirit that preserves the Apostolic faith in living and free experience, has an immense opportunity of serving the universal Church in this crisis of its history. It is with the vision of this possibility, and in the hope that in what remains to me of life, I may humbly help to realize it, that I end these Reminiscences, with the expression of thankfulness to God that, in spite of all my unworthiness, hitherto He has helped me. ' This God is our God for ever and ever. He will be our guide even unto death.'